Mammals of the
Canadian Rockies

Mammals of the Canadian Rockies

George W. Scotter
and Tom J. Ulrich

FIFTH
HOUSE
PUBLISHERS

Cover photograph by Wayne Lynch
Cover design by John Luckhurst/GDL

Printed in Canada
01 02 03 04 05/ 5 4 3 2

Canadian Cataloguing in Publication Data

Scotter, G.W. (George Wilby)
Mammals of the Canadian Rockies
Includes bibliographical references and index.
ISBN 1-895618-55-X

1. Mammals–Rocky Mountains, Canadian (B.C. and Alta.)–Identification.*
I. Ulrich, Tom J.
II. Title.
QL721.5.R63S36 1995   599.09711 C94-920276-2

Contents

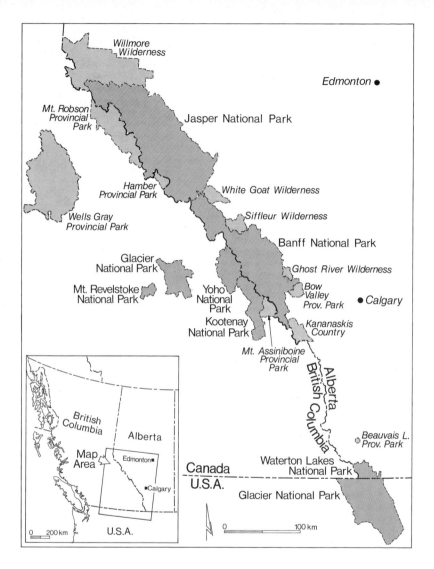

Figure 1. The southern portion of the Canadian Rocky Mountains and nearby areas.

Figure 2. The northern portion of the Canadian Rocky Mountains and nearby areas.

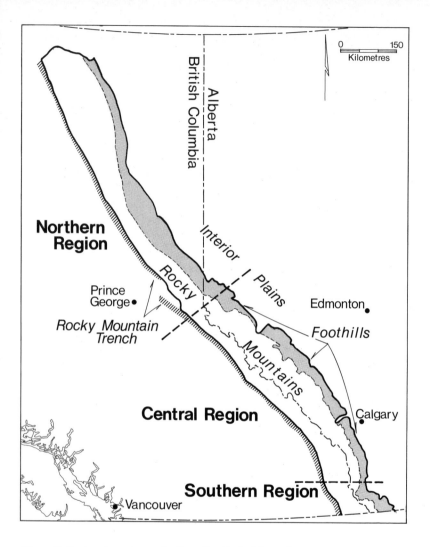

Figure 3. Regions in and near the Canadian Rocky Mountains.

Acknowledgements

We owe a debt of gratitude to a number of colleagues who contributed to this book. Parts of the manuscript were read and many useful suggestions were made by Etta Scotter, Lawson Sugden, Lu Carbyn, Bill Wishart, Don Thomas, Jan Edmonds, Steve Herrero, and Val Geist. Colleagues provided several photographs for the book; they are acknowledged in the photo credits. Regional checklists of mammals were updated by David Nagorsen (northern British Columbia), Ron Chamney (Kananaskis Country), Heather Dempsey and Robert Haney (Banff National Park), Larry Halverson (Kootenay National Park), Kevin Van Tighem (Yoho National Park), Jim Todgham (Jasper National Park), and Rob Watt (Waterton Lakes National Park). Special appreciation goes to Etta Scotter and Mona Adams for typing the manuscript.

Dedicated to those who appreciate the wonder and beauty of creatures in the wild. May the wild mammals of the Canadian Rockies give color and life to your outdoor experience and a welcome touch to your day.

Introduction

Millions of North Americans of all ages and from all walks of life are devoted to wildlife watching. This book supplies residents and visitors in the Canadian Rockies with what they need to know to start identifying and understanding the rich array of wild mammals that reside here, an absorbing hobby that can last a lifetime and springboard them into deeper studies. Learning about the creatures you see in alpine meadows, dark spruce forests, or arid grasslands can turn a pleasant walk through the muffled whisperings of nature into a fascinating adventure.

The Canadian Rockies provide habitat for some of the most magnificent mammals in North America. Grizzly bears still roam freely in the alpine meadows, wapiti feed in the forests, cougars stalk the watercourses and high country. In spite of humankind, the wolf still survives throughout the Rockies. Less spectacular but more numerous than their dramatic relatives, smaller mammals maintain a vital place within the ecosystems of the Canadian Rockies. Even the tiny shrew gains in stature when we appreciate the sophisticated mechanisms and behavior that regulate its life.

The purpose of *Mammals of the Canadian Rockies* is to help identify the mammals you are most likely to see and to describe their life histories. We hope this book will foster a greater interest in mammals, that it will help users to know them better and to develop a wider appreciation of nature, as well as a deeper understanding of the environment we share with these wild creatures within this striking segment of the Canadian landscape. This sense of connection with other life forms will profoundly affect the way we act and the demands we place on our shared world.

The Canadian Rockies

The Canadian Rocky Mountains (figures 1 and 2) are the northern segment of a large mountain system widely known for its rugged vistas. In Canada, the Rockies extend nearly 1400 km (870 mi) from the American border at the 49th parallel to the Liard River, flanked on the west by the Rocky Mountain Trench and on the east by the Interior Plains (figure 3).

The Canadian Rockies are aligned northwest-southeast and divisible into ranges. The foothills on the eastern boundary, 25 to 50 km wide (15 to 30 mi), rise above the Interior Plains as linear ridges and hills of Mesozoic shale and sandstone, and the Rocky Mountain Trench to the west marks a major fault line distinctly visible on satellite photos. The Muskwa Ranges of the northern Rocky Mountains are broadest and highest around Mount Sylvia [2942 m (9650 ft) in elevation] near Kwadacha Wilderness Provincial Park. The terrain in that area is as rugged as any other part of the Rockies, having been carved by glaciation from great sections of stratified rock. A number of glaciers continue to quarry the highest peaks.

The Rockies are narrow where crossed by the Peace River. To the south, the Hart Ranges rise gradually and form a relatively subdued terrain, with summits under 2750 m (9020 ft) in elevation. The Continental Ranges are linear, with great cliffs and precipitous faces of bare gray rock sculpted by glaciation from thick sections of limestone and dolomite. They are broad, and their summit elevations increase to that of the highest peak, Mount Robson (3954 m, 12970 ft), west of Jasper in Mount Robson Provincial Park. A number of high peaks on the Continental Divide cluster around the Columbia Icefield, the largest of many glaciers in the Rockies. Southward, peaks up to 3600 m (11800 ft) in elevation occur at intervals or in groups along the mountain backbone through the Banff area to Crowsnest Pass, south of which they are generally lower. Gadd (1995) provides an excellent outline of the geology and geography for the interested reader.

Within the Canadian Rockies, thousands of hectares of native mammal habitat are preserved and protected in areas such as Glacier-Waterton International Peace Park, four national parks, many provincial parks, a few wilderness areas such as White Goat and Willmore, and wildlife refuges such as Wilmer, north of Invermere, British Columbia.

Life Zones and Habitats

At first glance the trees and forests of the southern Canadian Rocky Mountains look like a continuous green carpet rolling up the mountainsides. Closer inspection reveals three major zones (biomes), each with its own characteristic plants and animals. These zones form bands across the mountainsides—somewhat like the layers of a wedding cake. The bottom band, called the montane, is found in the valley bottoms. The subalpine forms the middle layer, while the upper band, the alpine, is the land above the trees. One zone merges into another and there is much overlapping because of different topography, exposure, moisture, soil, and prevailing winds.

The nature enthusiast who learns to recognize these zones will soon realize that certain animals and plants can be expected to be found in a specific zone. This knowledge will help you discover the species you wish to see.

The more or less distinct altitudinal zonation is due, in part, to the gradual lowering of temperature from the lowland to the summit of a mountain. Thus, the lower part of most mountains is densely wooded, whereas the upper part may be treeless. At higher elevations, the trees become more stunted, and the upper limit of trees, or timberline, is generally quite distinct. Timberline is at about 2400 m (7874 ft) in the south, 2100 m (6890 ft) at Jasper, and 1500 m (4920 ft) in the north. On the warmer, south side of a mountain, timberline is often several hundred meters higher than on the cooler, more shaded north side.

Precipitation also greatly affects mammal distribution and the plant cover of mountains. Thus, the eastern foothills situated in the rain shadow of the mountains may be treeless and inhabited by drought-resistant prairie species, while the western foothills in British Columbia are covered with trees. Precipitation usually increases with altitude. This explains why some of the richest and most lush assemblages of vegetation may be found in sheltered alpine valleys above timberline. The plants are well protected by a deep blanket of snow in winter and abundantly supplied with water from melting snowbanks in summer. Another characteristic of the eastern slopes is the warm chinook wind that can melt the snow cover several times during a winter, making the vegetation available to mammals.

Several habitats and habitat complexes are found within these major vegetation zones, each with its characteristic mammals. Habitats within the Canadian Rockies are unusually variable, ranging from rich riparian areas to glacier-covered alpine slopes.

Plant and animal species form a continuum through these life zones. Some mammals are more or less characteristic of a particular life zone, such as mountain goats in the alpine and the striped skunk in the montane. Other mammals, such as coyotes, grizzly bears, and wapiti, have broad environmental requirements, and you may see them in any of the life zones. Some mammals may find their requirements met in restricted areas of a single life zone. Knowing a mammal's habitat requirements can help you identify unfamiliar species. The

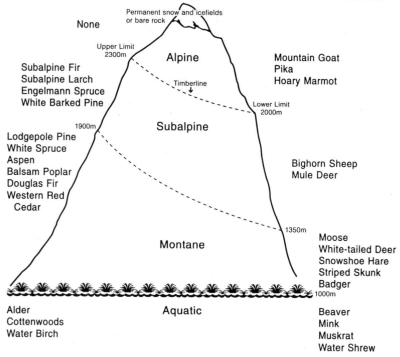

Characteristic Trees

None

Subalpine Fir
Subalpine Larch
Engelmann Spruce
White Barked Pine

Lodgepole Pine
White Spruce
Aspen
Balsam Poplar
Douglas Fir
Western Red
Cedar

Alder
Cottenwoods
Water Birch

Characteristic Mammals

Mountain Goat
Pika
Hoary Marmot

Bighorn Sheep
Mule Deer

Moose
White-tailed Deer
Snowshoe Hare
Striped Skunk
Badger

Beaver
Mink
Muskrat
Water Shrew

Permanent snow and icefields or bare rock

Upper Limit 2300m

Alpine

Timberline

Lower Limit 2000m

1900m

Subalpine

1350m

Montane

Aquatic

1000m

Figure 4. Life zones of the Canadian Rocky Mountains with examples of characteristic trees and mammals.

badger, for example, lives primarily in grassy habitats in the montane zone. When you see a badgerlike mammal on a scree slope in the subalpine zone, therefore, you can be reasonably sure it is not a badger. Other mammals inhabit specific ecological niches. Beaver and muskrat, for example, are seldom found far from water. But even in the same watery habitat, each species feeds, dens, moves, and mates in a unique way.

The major life zones in the Canadian Rocky Mountains are shown in figure 4; brief descriptions follow.

Montane Zone

The montane zone occurs at the lowest elevations in the southern Canadian Rockies at about 1000 m (3280 ft) above sea level. Its upper elevations vary, depending on location and aspect. The upper boundary, for example, is 1900 m (6235 ft) on warm southerly and westerly aspects in Kootenay National Park, and about 1350 m (4430 ft) in Jasper National Park.

The forests of the montane zone, in the southern Rockies, are generally dominated by Douglas fir and white spruce, which often follow the fire-

4

induced lodgepole pine and aspen trees. On some dry sites, however, lodgepole pine form forests that are not replaced by other trees. Balsam poplar, alder, willows, and birches frequent the moist areas, while western red cedar, western larch, and the occasional ponderosa pine are present in southeastern British Columbia.

Grasslands form the mature vegetation on the driest montane sites, and fire appears to be important in maintaining these areas as grasslands. Fescue grasslands, dominated by rough fescue and secondary quantities of Parry oat grass, occur in the foothills and valley bottoms on the eastern side of the Rocky Mountains. Further north, the grasslands are dominated by northern wheatgrass, June grass, and plains reed grass, while southeastern British Columbia is characterized mainly by wheatgrass communities.

Numerous shrubs are found in this zone, especially Canadian buffalo berry, common juniper, creeping juniper, snowberry, silverberry, prickly rose, wild gooseberry, bracted honeysuckle, saskatoon, red osier dogwood, shrubby cinquefoil, chokecherry, bearberry, and various willows. Shrubs become more abundant as moisture increases, usually occurring in suitable niches on north-facing slopes, in ravines, and in ground-water seepage areas.

Many wildflowers typical of the foothills and prairies are also present in the montane zone. Some of these are the nodding onion, wild gaillardia, wild flax, blue clematis, red and white baneberry, northern bedstraw, three-flowered avens, shooting star, western meadow rue, star-flowered Solomon's seal, common fireweed, pearly everlasting, blue beardtongue, asters, fleabanes, goldenrods, hedysarums, paintbrushes, and vetches, among many others [see Scotter and Flygare (1986) for details of individual wildflowers].

Typical mammals of the montane zone include the badger, snowshoe hare, and striped skunk. White-tailed deer and moose, while characteristic of the zone, occasionally move to subalpine and even alpine zones for brief periods. Other mammals such as mule deer and wapiti make greater use of the montane zone during the winter when snow is deep at higher elevations.

Extensive wetland complexes have developed along flood plains and are characterized by a mosaic of alders, birches, cottonwoods, cattails, pond weeds, willow fens, and sedge meadows. Such habitats are particularly important for water-loving mammals such as beaver and muskrat.

Subalpine Zone

The subalpine zone receives more rain and snow than the montane zone and hence supports a heavier growth of coniferous trees. Located above the montane zone and below the unforested alpine zone, the subalpine zone can be further divided into lower and upper subalpine. The predominant vegetation of the lower subalpine is a dense, closed coniferous forest. Mature forests are dominated by Engelmann spruce and subalpine fir. Lodgepole pine forests are also common at lower altitudes.

The upper subalpine portion, characterized by open forests and meadows, is intermediate between lower subalpine closed forest and treeless alpine tundra. Compared with the lower subalpine, the upper subalpine climate is cooler and wetter, with greater snowfall, later snowmelt, and a shorter growing season. High winds also appear to be a significant climatic factor, pruning the trees into characteristic stunted forms called "elfin wood" or *krummholz*. The only tree to escape this stunting is the deciduous subalpine larch, occurring from Lake Louise south within our area.

In the lower subalpine the trees grow so tall and so close together that little light reaches the forest floor. The ground vegetation consequently consists of a thick carpet of feather mosses and lichens. There are scatterings of shade-tolerant shrubs like white-flowered rhododendron, grouseberry, huckleberry, false huckleberry, and green alder. Shrubs of the heather family, such as white mountain heather, red heather, and yellow heather, are common in the more open forests near treeline. Some of the characteristic herbaceous plants include bronze bells, bunchberry, one-flowered clintonia, twinflower, and several wintergreens.

Characteristic mammals of the subalpine zone include the mule deer, bighorn sheep, Columbian ground squirrel, golden-mantled ground squirrel, and a few shrews and voles. Several other mammals inhabit the area, especially during the summer months, and caribou use the zone during midwinter because tree lichens are available for food.

Alpine Zone

Between the coniferous forest and the barren rocky peaks of the mountains is a zone in which herbaceous plants exist but which cannot support trees of any significant size. This is the alpine zone. It is colder, more exposed to wind, and receives heavier precipitation than the other zones. Tree growth is discouraged by a combination of long, cold winters, short, cool summers, and high winds. Vegetation is characterized by a mosaic of low shrub and herb communities in the lower alpine zone, and by lichens and xerophytic mosses, which are able to withstand extreme temperature fluctuation and desiccation, in the upper alpine zone. There is little or no vascular vegetation growing at the highest elevations.

Dwarf shrub tundra dominated by yellow heather, white mountain heather, arctic willow, and white mountain avens is characteristic of lower alpine altitudes. Dense mats of sedge prevail in depressions where the snow is deep in winter and melts late in the spring.

Many of the plants have special growth forms to take advantage of the heat and moisture available to them. These include prostrate forms growing along the surface of the ground; cushion plants that wedge themselves in crevices; and leathery or hairy-leaved forms, which conserve water by reducing the desiccation caused by wind. The shortness of the growing season and the severity of winter favor fast-growing perennials. Such hardy plants comprise the truly alpine and arctic element of the flora.

A few of the more conspicuous species in the alpine zone are purple saxifrage, moss campion, alpine rockcress, mountain sorrel, alpine lousewort, contorted lousewort, and the shrubs already mentioned. Some subalpine wildflowers find their way into the low alpine zone, as do several shrubs.

Few large ungulates are characteristic of the alpine zone on a year-round basis. The mountain goat is an exception, often facing the rigors of winter there. Other mammals, such as bighorn sheep, grizzly bear, wapiti, and mule deer, inhabit the alpine zone during more favorable times of the year, but they are more at home in subalpine and montane forests. Several smaller mammals, such as the hoary marmot, pika, water shrew, and northern red-backed vole, inhabit the alpine zone yearlong.

Mammals

With about five thousand species, just over 10 percent of all known vertebrates, mammals are not the most numerous animals, but they are the most dominant on this earth. The first mammals are believed to have evolved about 200 million years ago, during the Mesozoic Era. For more than 100 million years, however, mammals were eclipsed by reptiles, particularly the large dinosaurs. Some 70 million years ago, the dinosaurs came to an abrupt and mysterious end. The mammals had the necessary adaptations that allowed them to survive in the conditions that caused the demise of the dinosaurs, and became the dominant life forms. In the ensuing Age of Mammals, they flourished and diversified, filling hundreds of niches with numerous forms. Today, mammals are a diverse group of animals found in every habitat and climate from polar regions to tropics. Mammals live in every environment from oceans, bodies of fresh water, mountains, plains, and forests, to deserts. There are mammals that swim, fly, and burrow in the ground, each one ideally suited to its respective habitat.

What Are Mammals?

One of the most advanced adaptations of mammals is that they are warm-blooded; that is, they are able to maintain a relatively constant body temperature regardless of the outside temperature. The majority of mammals have a body temperature of between 36°C (97°F) and 40°C (104°F). A constant, high body temperature is necessary for the organs within the body to work efficiently. Unlike reptiles, which become inactive in cold conditions, most mammals remain active even in extreme environmental conditions, enabling them to colonize cooler areas of the earth. Some survive cold winter conditions by going into a state of suspended activity called hibernation. In others, internal mechanisms can trigger shivering, which works the muscles and generates metabolic heat. To combat excessive heat, mammals may be active only during cooler times of the day, shed hair, pant, sweat, burrow underground, or rest under a protective cover of shrubs or trees. The sweat glands, used to prevent overheating, are unique to this class.

Hair is as characteristic of mammals as feathers are for birds. This easily observed trait is discussed in a separate section because it is critically important to the survival of northern mammals.

The way mammals give birth to live young and take care of them is extremely important to their success. Mammals develop inside the female in a specialized structure called the uterus. The unborn young are thus more protected from predators than are eggs. A pregnant mammal has a chance to get away from a predator and, if she does, she saves not only herself but also her developing offspring.

Female mammals produce milk for their young in special glands, an ability that is a singular characteristic of this class. The word mammal comes from the Latin *mamma*, which means breast or nipple. Not all mammals have breasts, but almost all have one pair of teats or nipples on which the young suck to obtain milk for nourishment in the early stages of life.

All mammals in the Canadian Rockies are placental. Placental mammals develop in the uterus and receive their nourishment through a structure called the placenta. Although the young are born helpless, they are in a much higher state of development than is the case with egg-laying and pouched mammals.

Mammals give more care to their young than other forms of animal life. Much mammalian parental behavior is instinctive, but many also plan their actions, exercise choices, and teach their young survival skills. The length of time mammals take care of their young varies from a few days in some rodents to several months in grizzly bears. The care given by mammals makes up for their relatively low rates of reproduction, and their young have a much better chance for survival because of this parental care.

In general, the larger the mammal, the longer the gestation period and the smaller the number of offspring. The gestation period of the caribou, for example, is 7-8 months, and 1 calf is the usual result. In contrast, house mice have a gestation period of 21 days and produce several litters a year containing as many as 12 offspring each.

In addition to being warm-blooded, having hair, and the ability to produce milk, mammals have a number of other shared characteristics. They have four basic types of teeth: incisors, canines, premolars, and molars. The teeth of other vertebrates are not generally distinguishable into types. Mammalian teeth differ greatly with feeding habits. Because the number and shape of teeth vary between orders, these differences form a basis for the classification of mammals. Mammals have four-chambered hearts, lungs for breathing, diaphragms, seven neck vertebrae (with some exceptions), four feet, and highly developed nervous systems. Their sophisticated brain functions because the required oxygen supply is ensured by the four-chambered heart, diaphragm, and lungs. Their sense of hearing, sight, smell, and touch are extremely sensitive; mammals are the only vertebrates with three internal ear bones to enhance hearing. Another peculiarity of the mammal body is the epiglottis, a cartilaginous flap that closes the larynx, allowing breathing to occur simultaneously with swallowing.

The relatively large, highly developed brain, resulting in greater mental ability, is a basic characteristic of the whole mammalian class. Some mammals are capable of sophisticated activities such as coordinating the hunting of prey. Wolves, for example, hunt in groups and exercise what seems to be carefully developed strategy. The behavior of mammals, some of which may even be able to reason and solve problems, is more often guided by intelligence than any other class of animals.

A few other characteristics of mammals and their lifestyles, such as antlers and horns, color variations, communication, hair and fur, locomotion, and winter survival, should be considered.

Antlers and Horns

It is a popular misconception that antlers and horns are the same thing. There are a number of significant differences.

Permanent appendages that are not shed annually, horns are outgrowths of the frontal bones of the skull, with the frontal sinus actually extending into the core of each horn. A network of blood vessels carries nutrients and oxygen to the bone. Over this layer of blood vessels is a hard keratin sheath, the same protein that forms human fingernails. The keratinous sheath continues to grow throughout the life of the animal.

Horns occur in both sexes, although those of the male are generally larger and longer than those of the female. Horns are used in defense of the young and in battles to determine dominance among males. The powerful charges and head-butting of bighorn sheep rams as they determine their rank and status in the band are among the most spectacular animal confrontations in the Canadian Rockies.

In contrast, antlers, unlike horns, are deciduous. Like the leaves of the aspen tree, they grow and are shed on a yearly cycle, a phenomenon closely related to the male's sex life. Antlers grow from pedicels that extend from the frontal bones of the skull, and consist of bone with a mosslike covering appropriately called "velvet." That covering of spongy tissue is chock-full of blood vessels and protected by a mass of short hair. At first, the antlers are so soft that they are easily bent or broken. As the peak of sexual activity or "rut" approaches, antler growth ceases, the blood vessels in the velvet constrict, and the skin begins to die and fall away. Males thrash the vegetation to strip the drying velvet from the antlers and to polish them. Antlers, therefore, are living tissue during part of the year and nonliving at the end of their cycle.

Antlers grow at an astonishing rate. During the peak of the cycle, antler growth is more than 1.5 cm (0.6 in) a day, faster than any other bone. Enormous stores of minerals are required to make these lavish appendages. Hormonal triggering removes calcium and phosphorus from the male's ribs, sternum, and skull to fortify new antler growth. The size and number of points on the headgear relate to both diet and the animal's age.

Antlers are sex symbols or ornaments to attract females rather than weapons for fighting or protection. They are badges of masculinity used to establish dominance among males through wrestling and fighting during the rut. The more dominant males will breed with the greatest number of females, thereby preserving their gene pools.

After the breeding season the males cannot afford to be encumbered with such extravagant headgear. The racks drop off in the face of winter, when snow and hunger make the males especially vulnerable to predators. The storehouse of nutrients in the antlers is seldom wasted, however; you will rarely find discarded antlers that have not been chewed by other animals. Rodents, in particular, gnaw on dropped antlers, deriving useful minerals from them and also wearing down their incisors in the process.

Regardless of whether they are secondary sex characteristics, symbols of status, or functional lines of defense, antlers and horns add grace, power, and majesty to their bearers.

Color Variations

Many mammals have color variations because of age, sex, time of the year, and their environment. Fawns of both species of deer found in the Canadian

Rockies, for example, are born dappled with spots on the sides and top of their coat that disappear within weeks. Bison calves are born with an orangy brown, crinkled coat, and within ten weeks molt into a brown, juvenile coat. White-tailed deer have a reddish fawn dorsal summer coat, often called the "red coat." Their winter coat is longer, stiffer, and a grizzled gray in color. This coat is referred to as the "blue coat." Snowshoe hares and weasels change the color of their coat with the seasons to match that of the landscape. The neck hair and mane of male caribou are long and creamy white during the winter, with the color often extending across the lower shoulders and flanks. These characteristics are less developed in female caribou.

Remember also that not all black bears are black and not all red foxes are red. Black bears, in fact, may be brown, cinnamon, or blonde. It is not uncommon for an array of colors to be present in the same litter of foxes. Phases other than red include black, silver, and mixed colors.

On rare occasions you may see an individual animal that is much darker or lighter than normal. This quirk results from the mutation of a single gene that controls the manufacture of a protein pigment called melanin, which gives color to the hair and skin. Overproduction of melanin will conceal all other colors, resulting in a melanistic or black animal. Albinistic or white animals result from the absence of melanin. Melanin is important in protecting the skin cells, underlying blood vessels, and connective tissue from the harmful effects of ultraviolet light. Albino animals, therefore, are especially susceptible to skin cancer.

Although albinism and melanism occur at about the same rate in nature, the incidence varies among species. Neither are uncommon, for example, in squirrels.

Not all white animals are true albinos. In winter the pelts of snowshoe hares and weasels turn white. They can be distinguished from true albinos by the presence of darkly pigmented eyes.

Albino mammals may have a disadvantage in survival against dark backgrounds, but an advantage against lighter backgrounds, particularly in snow. The reverse is likely true of melanistic mammals.

Communication

Most mammals in the Canadian Rockies are not particularly notable for their vocal repertoire. They do communicate, however, by a variety of scents, sounds, visual signals, and touch.

Many mammals use sound in the process of mating, hunting, socializing, migrating, and in staking out or defending territories. Vocalization is most common during the breeding season. The piercing bugle of wapiti bulls and the guttural bellow of bull bison are striking examples of sounds made during the rut. Both species make other calls as well. An alarm "bark," for example, is made by both sexes of wapiti to indicate potential danger, and separated wapiti cows and calves produce a squeal until they are reunited. Many other mammals produce specific sounds unique to their species.

Most mammals warn others away with a harsh, low-pitched growl, low-frequency sounds apparently making the growler seem larger and more threatening. In contrast, mammals use high-pitched sounds to show amiability or submissiveness, this type of call making the producer seem smaller and less threatening. Tonal sounds are also used for mother-offspring interactions and in some courtship displays. Research suggests that some animal sounds are genetically programmed, while others are learned from their elders.

Some mammals produce sound at frequencies too low for humans to hear. Such low-frequency calls travel long distances and pass intact through obstructions. These long-distance communication systems need further study as little is understood about their function.

Smell has a profound importance in the daily life of mammals. Chemical signals advertise dominance, reproductive status, and territorial boundaries. And chemical signals, unlike sounds, have the advantage of persisting.

Carnivores use their sense of smell to find food and to communicate with each other. Wolves, for example, can smell prey that is not visible. They can also follow a trail that is not fresh. Male carnivores taste the urine of females to determine those in a receptive state for breeding. Most carnivores scentmark their territory with urine and glandular secretions to establish their dominance. Members of the cat family mark their territory by spraying urine widely over vegetation rather than marking single spots like members of the dog family. Cats also rub their cheeks on the ground, leaving a trail of glandular secretion.

Ungulates possess a variety of scent glands. Both species of deer in the Canadian Rockies have four sets of scent glands: the preorbital gland near the front of the eye, tarsal glands on the hocks, metatarsal glands on the lower legs, and interdigital glands between the toes. Mountain goats have well-developed glands at the base of their horns. Secretions from scent glands serve a variety of functions such as establishing territories, allowing animals to retrace their tracks in unfamiliar terrain, advertising their presence, locating mates during the breeding season, and helping dams to locate and identify their young.

Visual signals, such as an array of postures, displays, and threats, impart information within a mammal's community. The position of antlers or horns, ears, eyes, head and neck, and body size can be used in both threat and submissive displays. Other visual signals indicate danger. The inflated white rump-patches in alarmed pronghorn antelope and the warning tail flash of white-tailed deer are typical examples.

Tactile communications can include nose touching, nudging, licking or rubbing the face or body of dominant animals, head or chin resting on mate's back, symbolic biting, and many others. With such threatening or appeasing gestures, a mammal often gets its point across without violence. Because fatal fights are costly affairs, many mammals have evolved with behavioral and anatomical adaptations that help to solve disputes without too much damage.

Hair and Fur

When hair is dense and covers much of a mammal's body, it is called fur. Fur is a rather broad term, covering many different types of hair. Mammal fur is usually made up of two distinct kinds of hair, an outer coat of long, coarse guard hairs, with an inner coat of short, fine underhairs. Hair gives color and contour to an animal, but more important is its value as insulation and protection.

The most obvious and clearly visible hair is the coarse guard hair—long, pigmented, durable hairs meant to take abrasion and weathering. The guard hairs of most mammals have a narrow base and a flattened tip. Some guard hairs are modified; porcupine quills are a good example. Some members of the cat and dog families have erector muscles that raise the guard hairs to make the animal look larger and more ferocious when threatened.

If you were to spread the guard hairs, you would reveal a soft underfur. The underfur may be extremely fine, downy hairs (velus); short, dense, and fine; or woolly. These hairs have one major purpose, that of retaining heat. The insulation value is a function of both the density and length of the hair. Northern mammals usually have both a winter and summer coat, with much of the underfur being shed each spring and replaced by a thinner, cooler coat in summer. In the fall, the fine hairs grow dense again for winter. Since guard hairs do not change much during the year, an animal's healthy appearance in the winter is due, in part, to the full growth of underfur.

Another type of hair is found on antelope and on most members of the deer family. Their pelage consists of thick, hollow guard hairs with only a sparse covering of underfur. You will often see wapiti or deer with a substantial layer of frost on their backs in winter, but the insulation factor of the thick, hollow hairs is so great that the animals are not affected by the frost. In water, the hollow hair adds buoyancy to some animals, such as caribou, and assists them in swimming.

The high quality of furs available in North America spawned the fur trade that resulted in the discovery and exploration of much of Canada, including the Rockies.

Locomotion

Looking at the footprints or tracks of mammals can tell us something about their locomotion and the long evolutionary development of the foot. It can help us understand why some animals are faster than others.

Primitive mammals have five toes on each foot, both fore and aft. A large group, these mammals take their steps by placing the heel first, planting the whole foot, then stepping away on the ball of the foot. This is a slow, time-consuming process not conducive to speed. The bear, badger, porcupine, and skunk all travel by this method. They are called "plantigrade" (figure 5), as are humans.

Through evolution, some mammals have picked their heels off the ground. You can simulate the process by placing your palm down on a flat surface. This is the plantigrade position. Keep your fingers on the surface and slowly raise your palm, bending at the joint of the fingers. Notice the thumb or fifth digit also leaves the surface. This is the "digitigrade" position of modern mammals. Animals save a considerable amount of time by walking on their digits. The fox, bobcat, and wolf are digitigrade. Examine the front legs of your pet dog or cat

Plantigrade   Digitigrade   Unguligrade

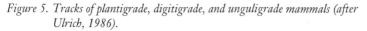

Figure 5. Tracks of plantigrade, digitigrade, and unguligrade mammals (after Ulrich, 1986).

to see the remnant thumb or dewclaw on the inside of each leg. This is typical of digitigrade mammals.

Returning to your hand with the palm raised, bring the fingers up so just the tips remain touching. This is the "unguligrade" position, with only the tips of the toes on the ground. The fifth digit has completely disappeared on animals in this group. The first and fourth digits rise to become dewclaws, while the last two develop enlarged nails or hoofs. Deer, wapiti, moose, and caribou walk on their nails. These ungulates are built for speed.

In addition to stance, the mode of progression or gait has evolved. Primitive mammals were probably walkers (ambulatory). Larger mammals in open habitats needed to be swift runners (cursorial) to escape predators. In the same habitats, smaller mammals are often jumpers (saltatorial). Some became swimmers (natatorial), some became climbers (scansorial) to invade the trees, and the bats developed the capability of true, powered flight (volant). The diversity of locomotor adaptations was possible because of the highly plastic nature of the mammalian body.

By studying the tracks left by mammals, the outdoor traveler can tell much about what has happened in an area. Tracks can tell what animals have passed through the area, how many there were, how long ago they were present, the direction of travel, whether the animals were running or moving slowly, perhaps what they were doing, and much more. Since many mammals are furtive, usually silent, and often active at night, "reading" the story left by their passage can tell us much about their complex world. Murie (1975) prepared an excellent field guide to animal tracks.

Winter Survival

Snow and bitterly cold weather during the winter are critical factors for all resident mammals in the Canadian Rockies. Snow may be meters deep at higher elevations and can remain for months. The snow not only covers food, but also impedes movement and depletes the limited energy reserve of many mammals. Unlike many birds that fly away to warmer climes, most mammals must stay and tough it out, each species in its own fashion. Let's briefly consider some of the marvelous winter adaptations that our resident animals use in their snow-shrouded environments.

A few mammals avoid the demands of winter by hibernating or sleeping. Hibernation, or the "little death" as it is sometimes called, permits animals the ultimate in energy conservation. Hibernators, such as jumping mice, ground squirrels, and some bats, spend the winter in a resting state with drastically lowered body temperature, heart rate, and breathing. In the ground squirrel, for example, the body temperature crashes from 36°C (97°F) to 4°C (39°F), heartbeat reduces from 250 beats per minute to 10, and respiration goes from 100 breaths per minute to about 4. Although the energy stored as body fat from the frenzied feeding of the summer will maintain most hibernators until spring, weight losses of 30 to 40 percent may be sustained.

Other mammals, such as bears, chipmunks, raccoons, and skunks, survive the ordeals of winter in a state of torpor or dormancy. Since their body functions remain nearly normal, they are best described as deep sleepers. Unlike true hibernators, deep sleepers can be wakened readily, and on mild days may sally forth to tend to their toiletries and nibble some food.

Small mammals, such as beavers and red squirrels, are active throughout the winter and instinctively prepare by storing food. Red squirrels cache large stores of cones from conifers and dry mushrooms for use when food is scarce. Beavers store food in underwater caches or in their burrows before they are locked within their ice-bound world.

For many small mammals most activities take place below the layers of snow. This subnivian environment provides more stable conditions and less temperature extremes than those prevailing above the insulating white layers. Under that blanket there is no wind to sweep away the body heat of small shrews or rodents. Deer mice use their stores of food, and in extreme cold crowd together in nests for warmth. Shrews, which do not store food, must hunt constantly in the undersnow environment to meet the demands of their insatiable appetites. Nor do they huddle together for warmth during the coldest weather, because one may become dinner for the other.

In lieu of snug dens, caves, underground refuges, or undersnow environments, some animals depend on their own physical adaptations to survive snow, severe blizzards, and numbing cold spells. Many mammals grow longer, thicker fur to trap dead air close to the skin, thereby providing greater insulation. Internal changes also help acclimatize some mammals to winter. More blood may be pumped to the paws, ears, tail, and nose when extra warmth is needed. Red fox, because of such changes, can survive winters that are 38°C (100°F) colder than their usual summer temperatures without undergoing cold stress. Bobcats, lynx, and snowshoe hares develop well-furred, snowshoelike paws to provide added maneuverability in the snow.

Some mammals that remain active all winter change the color of their coat to match the landscape. The coats of snowshoe hares and weasels turn from summer gray and brown to white with the early snows of winter, enabling them to blend into their surroundings. These camouflagelike transformations may render them less visible to potential enemies in the case of the snowshoe hare, and less readily detectable by their prey in the case of the weasel.

Some ungulates, particularly mule deer and herds of wapiti, descend into the montane valleys, where snowfalls are lighter and less frequent. Favored wintering sites are on sheltered southern slopes with aspen and grasslands nearby. Other ungulates are less affected by snow depth. Mountain caribou, for example, may move to treeline in midwinter to forage on tree lichens. They are able to cope with deep snow because of their unusually large foot size, which allows them either to walk on top of the snow or sink in only a small depth. Of the hooved mammals in the Rockies, caribou have the smallest "track loading." In other words, they are the lightest on their feet. Moose cope better than bison, deer, or wapiti in deep snow because of their longer legs. The increased clearance, or "chest height," means they can move in deeper snow without dragging their bellies in it, thus reducing the amount of energy lost while moving and feeding.

Recent studies suggest that some mammals, such as the white-tailed deer, have a strategy for energy conservation during the winter. They may concentrate in small areas, move more slowly, forage less, and be more lethargic. Many of their body functions drop to seasonal lows, which results in diminished demands on their limited energy reserves.

Despite all the marvelous adaptations and strategies for survival, some mammals do die from starvation and freezing during the winter months. Sometimes they perish in great numbers. Severe winters may reduce overpopulations of some mammals, but over the longer term the result is a rejuvenated population because of the removal of aged, crippled, injured, and sick individuals.

How to Use This Book

There are large hardback volumes and small field guides in which you could seek descriptions and identification of North American mammals. Few, however, are devoted to the Canadian Rockies or attempt to cover that region in detail. Others are written in technical terms, unlike this book, which is written for the lay person. Every effort has been made to simplify the presentation of the material, but still make it accurate, interesting, and understandable.

About 75 species of mammals occur in the Canadian Rockies. This book provides information on identification, status, distribution, and habitat for all of these species, except for humans. Several photographs of all the large, more visible mammals are included in this book, but only representative species of the smaller mammals are illustrated. Photographs of the latter were selected on the basis of species abundance, ease of identification, the likelihood of the casual observer encountering them, and on photograph availability. One or more photographs from each of the families of mammals regularly found in the region has been included.

For identification, we encourage the reader to use the photographs along with the text. For most mammals, the photographs will illustrate the basic features, and there is also detailed information in the text to confirm identification. Most of the photographs are of mammals in a characteristic pose in a natural setting, as they would normally be viewed at close range. Photographs closely resemble the way the human eye sees a mammal, so they add a dimension of realism and natural beauty. We also recognize the limitations of the photographic approach. Consequently, the reader may want to use this book in conjunction with the excellent atlases and books listed in the selected references.

Nomenclature generally follows *Alberta Mammals: An Atlas and Guide* by Smith (1993). We have departed from the convention of following the order of mammals from the simplest to the more complex, choosing instead to begin with the largest, most conspicuous mammals and progressing down to the smaller, less visible, but still interesting creatures.

For each mammal, the text includes reference to its common and scientific names, size and weight, key field marks, habitat preference, distinguishing behavioral characteristics, and other items of interest. There are full-color photographs throughout, each with appropriate text, providing an easy-to-use field guide to many of the common and most often seen mammals of the Canadian Rockies. The basic natural history information provides insights into the daily lives of these mammals. We hope to answer the many questions you may ask, such as, What is it? Where does it live? How does it survive the winter? What does it eat? Who eats it? Where are the young? Why does it act that way?

All known living animals and plants are arranged into a graded system based on physical resemblances. Every living thing belongs to a kingdom (animal or plant), a phylum, a class, an order, a family, a genus, and a species. The genus and species titles make up the formal name. These two-part names are comparable to the names of people belonging to different families. In scientific names, however, the first part tells the genus (group) to which the mammal belongs; for example, *Canus* means dog in Latin. This is the same as a surname or family name, such as Jones. The second part of the name indicates the species (particular member of the group); for example, *lupus*, which means wolf in Latin. This is comparable to the given name of an individual, such as Tom in Tom Jones. No two species share the same two-part scientific name. Mammalogists have not agreed on standard common names, which occasionally causes confusion. Current common names are used throughout the text, with an occasional reference to local and other names.

For all the species described and illustrated we have included observations about their distribution within the Canadian Rocky Mountains. For convenience, the Rockies are divided into three major regions: northern, central, and southern. The northern region includes the Rockies north of Jasper National Park; the central region from Highway 3 to the northern boundary of Jasper National Park; and the southern region from the international boundary to Highway 3 (figure 3). The Canadian Rockies are often referred to as simply "the Rockies" or "our area."

The distribution of mammals is generally well known in the southern and central regions, but little information is available for the north except for the economically important ungulates. Detailed studies of mammal abundance and distribution at Waterton (Nielsen, 1973), Yoho (McCrory and Blood, 1978), Banff and Jasper (Holroyd and Van Tighem, 1983), and Kootenay (Poll *et al.*, 1984) were consulted, along with personal experience, in making those assessments. For each mammal, we have given distributions for Banff (B), Jasper (J), Kananaskis Country (KC), Kootenay (K), Northern British Columbia (N), Waterton Lakes (W), and Yoho (Y). Distributions in other regions can be judged by their proximity to these areas.

Obvious distinctive features, which will aid in identifying each species of mammal, are given in the descriptions. We also make comparisons with similar species so users can watch for those characteristics that most readily distinguish one from the other. Field marks are the points to look for to distinguish quickly and accurately each species from others that closely resemble it. Special field marks such as rump patches, antler shape, and colored markings are also included. Many mammals have color variations because of age, sex, time of year, and their environment; the photographs illustrate many of these variations.

In conjunction with field marks, other factors such as sounds, habits, and habitat can be helpful in identifying mammals. It is also important to know where and when individual species normally occur, and their status in selected areas of the Canadian Rockies.

Since the process of locating a particular mammal is greatly simplified by knowing where to look, we have provided comments on the habitat preferences for each mammal described. Most of the small mammals are limited to a specific habitat by adaptations they have made to the physical and biological conditions found within that habitat or habitat complex. Larger mammals may have huge home ranges and travel long distances. Mammals in general, however, are not evenly distributed across their ranges. Some species are highly local and found only in specialized habitats. Muskrats, for example, are found near water. On the other hand, mountain goats require steep rocky slopes.

The carnivores and ungulates have great mobility and most can tolerate a variety of habitats. Mammals can be seen everywhere within the Canadian Rockies, so one should not be too surprised to find an animal entirely out of its normal habitat.

Every mammal will not be found on any given day at any given habitat. Wildlife watching is full of temporary disappointments and surprises. But it is always a challenge to find and identify mammals and other wildlife in their natural environment.

While our goal is to keep technical terminology to an absolute minimum, readers need to understand some basic biological terms. A glossary is therefore included.

For the user whose interest in mammals is more than casual, a checklist of all species found in the Canadian Rockies is appended. This list is accurate to the date of completion of the manuscript (December 1994).

If you are a novice wildlife watcher, the following may help improve your observations. Mammals tend to avoid noise and commotion. You will see many more animals if you and your companions walk quietly and speak softly. Remember also that various kinds of mammals are active during different times of the day. The best viewing time for most mammals is when the day is either still young or well advanced. During the rest of the day, many mammals are relatively sluggish and silent. A few, such as Richardson's ground squirrel, are easy to find throughout the day during the summer. Bats are active at night.

Beginners are also encouraged to become familiar with characteristic signs that can assist in identifying mammals in the field. Because mammals of the Rockies are mostly ground-dwellers, they leave signs such as tracks, trails, droppings, gnawings, scratches, rubbings, remnants of meals, burrows, dens, dams, nests, middens, haystacks, and others. By examining these signs, mammal enthusiasts can learn much about the animals in a specific area. The ability to identify mammals accurately and efficiently in the field improves with practice and experience.

If you want to become a serious wildlife watcher, notes on your observations are important. With practice, you will develop your own techniques for making quick and accurate observations—random bits of information often fit together like a puzzle to form a clear picture. There can be a great deal of pleasure in keeping a journal of what you see, and field notes can be supplemented with photographs, videos, and sound recordings. Such diaries and other records are important to ourselves and other nature lovers. Written observations of pioneers, for example, help us understand the distribution patterns of mammals over time, and may help to shed light on other important ecological questions. Wildlife watching is not only endlessly entertaining, but also wonderfully educational.

The color photographs, nontechnical descriptions, and convenient size will make this book useful to the backpacker, hiker, mountain climber, highway traveler, kitchen-window wildlife watcher, and the generally curious-minded. We will have succeeded if we can introduce you to some of the magnificent mammals waiting to be discovered in our Rocky Mountain inheritance. Few other areas of the world have such large, diverse, and healthy populations of native mammals and the vast wilderness habitats necessary for their support. Being able to identify the mammals you encounter is an indispensable and exciting first step toward a deeper understanding and appreciation of the natural world around you.

Cloven-Hoofed Ungulates

(Order *Artiodactyla*)

Deer (Family *Cervidae*)
Pronghorn (Family *Antilocapridae*)
Bovid (Family *Bovidae*)

The cloven-hoofed ungulates within the Canadian Rockies are highly variable in behavior and morphology. One of the things they have in common is an even number of weight-bearing toes. The third and fourth digits have elongated to form two, parted hoof lobes sheathed in a strong material. Toes two and· five (the dewclaws), reduced in size and higher on the legs, are used for support when the animals travel on muddy or soft ground. The first digit, equivalent to our big toe or thumb, is absent. Their cloven hoofs and long legs are designed for running, thereby assisting individuals to escape from predators.

All members of the cloven-hoofed ungulates are cud chewers and have a large, four-chambered stomach. This specialized digestive tract works in the following way: first, the individual uses its tongue to push vegetation against the lips and roof of the mouth, shearing it off with the lower teeth and grinding it with the molars. The forage is then passed to the rumen, the first pouch of the stomach, where bacteria and protozoans help break down the plant material. The cud is regurgitated and passed to the second chamber, the reticulum, for additional digesting. It is then regurgitated a second time and thoroughly chewed again. Finally, it is passed back through the rest of the digestive tract. Symbiosis between the microorganisms and the ruminant makes more nutrients available to the browsing (eating twigs of shrubs and trees) or grazing (eating forbs and grasses) mammal.

Identification of the three families of cloven-hoofed ungulates in the Canadian Rockies is relatively easy based on the characteristics of antlers or horns. Male caribou, mule deer, white-tailed deer, wapiti, and moose—members of the *Cervidae* family—have antlers of solid bone that are shed each year and grow anew. Female caribou may also have small antlers. In contrast, both sexes of bison, mountain goats, and mountain sheep—family *Bovidae*—have horns that grow continually and are not shed. The bone core is covered by a tough keratinous sheath, similar in composition to our fingernails. Both male and female pronghorn—the single member of the *Antilocapridae* family—have horns. While the outer sheath of agglutinized hair on pronghorn horns is shed and replaced each year, the bony core is retained for life.

The artiodactyls first appeared about 50 million years ago. There are approximately 180 species worldwide grouped into nine families, including several domesticated species such as cattle, goats, sheep, and swine. Members of this order range over a wide variety of habitats from open grasslands, alpine meadows, and rocky cliffs, to deep forests. In the Canadian Rockies we have 10 species representing three families. The pronghorn, however, is present only in the grasslands of extreme southwestern Alberta on an occasional basis.

Wapiti or Elk
Cervus elaphus

BJKCKNWY*

DEER FAMILY

Wapiti is a Shawnee Indian word meaning "light colored" or "white deer," an apparent reference to the animal's buff-colored rump, or the buckskin appearance of the males. Although more commonly called "elk," that name technically belongs to the European moose.

When European settlers first arrived in North America, wapiti were the most widespread member of the deer family. They were found everywhere except for the Atlantic coastal plain, a few southern states, and the Far North. The vast herds, not unlike the bison, vanished from the East and were in a precarious condition in most of western North America by 1900. In Yellowstone National Park, both protection and the systematic removal of predators allowed the herds of wapiti to grow. Yellowstone became the source herd for restocking many depleted ranges with the majestic wapiti. Banff and Jasper national parks received 361 wapiti between 1917 and 1920 to bolster their faltering herds. Wapiti are also native to northern Europe and Asia, and have been successfully introduced to other countries such as New Zealand.

The wapiti's most distinguishing features are its buff-colored rump patch shaped like a light bulb, and in the case of males, massive, branching antlers. In early winter, pelage on the sides is gray brown, in striking contrast to the blackish brown head and neck. Males also develop a shaggy mane on the neck. The pelage bleaches during the winter and is replaced by a short, more reddish, summer coat. The short tail is the same color as the rump patch. The hinds (females) usually show less contrasting coloration than the stags.

The rack of a prime stag is magnificent. Such a regal headdress may have a length of 1.5 m (4.9 ft), spreading well over the back; a span of 1.2 m (4 ft); and

* Indicates distribution. See "How to Use This Book," page 17, for explanation of letters.

WAPITI BULL / TOM J. ULRICH

23

weigh between 18 and 22 kg (40 and 48 lb). Each antler consists of a long main beam with branching tines or prongs. Unlike the other deer in the Canadian Rockies, wapiti stags carry their antlers through most of the winter. Some Asians believe powdered wapiti antler can serve as a general tonic and powerful aphrodisiac.

The size of the antlers depends on a stag's age, although there are variations depending on the nutritional status. A yearling will generally have a single spike. Four or five points may develop on each side during the second year, but

WAPITI COW WITH CALF / TOM J. ULRICH

WAPITI CALF / TOM J. ULRICH

the beams tend to be slender. By the third year, the number of tines may remain the same, but the antlers are more heavily beamed. In future years there may be six or more points. Hunters give the larger stags regal names such as "royal," "imperial," or "monarch," depending on the number of tines on an antler.

An adult stag is about 2.4 m (7.9 ft) in length, 1.4 m (4.6 ft) tall at the shoulder, and weighs from 300 to 350 kg (660 to 770 lb). The largest stags can push the scales to near 500 kg (1100 lb). Hinds are smaller and weigh an average of 225 kg (495 lb).

WAPITI BULL IN SNOW / TOM J. ULRICH

Wapiti carry vestigial upper canines that seem to serve no apparent purpose. They are known popularly as "buglers," "ivory," "eye" teeth, or "tusks." These canine teeth are highly prized for use as jewelry.

These mammals are the noisiest of our deer, communicating with each other through their bugling, squeals, barks, and bleats. The most familiar sound is the challenging bugle of a stag ringing through the forest during the rut. The "*A-a-a-ae-e-eeeeee-eough! E-hu, e-hu!*" sounds warn rivals of his presence. The high bugling sound may carry a kilometer or more on the clear, crisp autumn air. Hinds make loud barks or squeals as alarm notes; their calves bleat.

Sparring is not limited to stags. Antlerless hinds threaten each other by rearing on their back legs and flailing out with their sharp front hoofs, usually to establish social position within the herd.

Recent studies in the Canadian Rockies indicate that wapiti are extremely adaptable. Some hinds have annual home ranges of less than 20 km² (8 mi²), while others have home ranges up to 414 km² (160 mi²). Some animals never leave dense riverbottom forests; others move to higher elevations each spring, taking up summer residence in subalpine forests and alpine slopes. Some wapiti stay in a valley one summer and move to the high mountain slopes the next. Wapiti appear to have a strong fidelity to their seasonal habitats, rutting area, and calving grounds, returning to the same locations year after year.

Wapiti are sociable, herding animals; apart from the occasional stag, wapiti are seldom found alone.

These creatures are versatile in their choice of food as well. They eat the leaves of shrubs and broad-leaved herbaceous plants in the summer, mushrooms in the autumn, and a mixture of grasses, sedges, and fallen aspen leaves in the winter, when their diets are controlled largely by snow. When the snow is loose and shallow, wapiti dig craters to secure dry grasses and leaves. As the snow gets deeper or too hard to dig, they shift their diet to woody twigs.

The magic and madness of the rut is a spectacle never to be forgotten. By late August the stags' hard antlers are rubbed clean of velvet and the once-placid, cud-chewing ruminants are transformed into bellicose fighters. Access to hinds depends principally on fighting ability, which relates in turn to the animal's body size. The stag's body size is influenced by its growth as a juvenile, which appears to depend on its mother's milk yield. Thus, the future breeding success of a stag may be largely determined within the first few months after birth.

The rut of wapiti, based on male advertisement, is spectacular. Prime stags

WAPITI BULLS FIGHTING / TOM J. ULRICH

WAPITI COW IN WATER / TOM J. ULRICH

announce their presence with loud calls, by distributing scent, and by being visible. Their high-pitched bugle, ending in a shrill whistle, grunts, and barks, reverberates through the mountain valleys. They dig wallows into which they urinate, and then roll. They rub their long manes on the edge of the wallows and later rub the "perfumed," urine-soaked mud off their caked necks onto trees. Shrubs may also be rubbed with the antlers and marked with scent. This advertising is to attract as many females as possible and to daunt rivals. A sham battle, or a few intimidating gestures and calls, might scare off an intruder, although if a stag cannot intimidate a rival, he is not shy about fighting. Real battles tend to be short affairs. Charges are normally met antlers to antlers, and victorious stags are not reluctant to gore their weaker rivals on retreat. A mature stag may have 30 to 50 wounds on the neck, head, shoulders, and haunches by the end of the rutting season. The more successful harem masters may take charge of 20 or more hinds. This ensures the strongest traits will be passed on to future generations. The ability of a stag to breed successfully will probably last no more than four years.

Following the turmoil of the rut, the stags leave the females to forage and recoup their exhausted stores of body fat before the hardships of winter. For some stags, irretrievably depleted by the demands of the rut, only a new crop of calves will remain as their legacy the following spring. The survivors will renew themselves for the spectacle of the mating season ten months later.

In late May or early June, after a gestation period of about eight and one-half months, a single calf is born, weighing in at about 17 kg (37 lb); twins are rare. Russet-coated, with creamy dapples on the back and flanks, the calf is kept in seclusion for about three weeks, during which time it is particularly vulnerable to predators. In some areas, up to 50 percent of the calves are killed by

WAPITI BULL IN VELVET / TOM J. ULRICH

bears before the youngsters are strong enough for the hind and calf to rejoin the herd. In addition to humans, wolves, bears, and cougars are their main enemies. Collisions with cars on highways and with trains, particularly in parks, are also a major mortality factor. In some herds, mortality from these sources exceeds the annual increase from births. As a result, fencing and specially constructed underpasses for wildlife were built along the Trans-Canada Highway near the town of Banff. That program is saving wapiti, other wildlife, and humans from injury and death.

Recent studies of radio-collared wapiti suggest that extreme infestations of liver flukes may be causing the deaths of some animals. In other cases the infestation may weaken the animals and thus predispose them to capture by wolves or other predators.

Wapiti are highly prized as trophies of the hunt. In the management of wildlife resources outside of parks, certain wapiti populations can, and sometimes must, be culled to prevent excessive damage to crops, haystacks, and native vegetation. If managed wisely, a wapiti population will be maintained at the desired level for all concerned—the farmers and ranchers, the hunters, and those who just enjoy watching them.

These imposing animals are common on the eastern slopes from the Willmore Wilderness Park south, and on the western slopes from Yoho National Park south. They are occasionally seen in the northern Rockies. Wapiti are often visible from the highways in many of the mountain parks, and in the autumn you should hear the mountains resonate with their haunting mating calls. Wapiti within some national parks are tolerant of humans, stags with their harems often being seen within the towns of Banff and Jasper. Beware, however, as a stag in rut can be extremely dangerous. He may consider you a rival for his harem!

Mule Deer

Odocoileus hemionus

BJKCKNWY

DEER FAMILY

The mule deer, or "muley" as it is often called, is a westerner. It evolved in the dry, rugged badlands and mountains of western North America. Several distinct forms of this deer range from Alaska and the extreme southern Yukon and Northwest Territories to northern Mexico and the Baja Peninsula, and from Manitoba to the West Coast. In contrast, the white-tailed deer evolved in the deciduous forest areas of the eastern portion of North America. The ranges of the two species now overlap rather broadly in the West and hybrids are known to occur.

The mule deer owes its common name to explorers William Clark and Meriwether Lewis, who compared its ears to those of a mule. It has huge, broad, black-fringed ears that swivel constantly from side to side and are at least two-thirds the length of its head.

The best characteristics for positive identification of the mule deer are its tail and the antlers of bucks from summer to midwinter. The 20 cm (8 in) long,

MULE DEER BUCK / TOM J. ULRICH

29

narrow tail of a mule deer is white with a black tip. In contrast, the white-tailed deer has a much bushier tail that is white but without the black tip. When alarmed and moving, the mule deer generally holds its tail horizontal or down, while white-tailed deer, especially females and young, hold their tails erect and wagging like a flag. The tines of a buck mule deer's antlers extend upward from the main beam and then fork into a Y. Each arm of the Y may fork again depending on the age, size, and nutritional status of the buck. Typical whitetail antlers have single tines that extend from the tops of the main beams and do not fork.

Also distinctive is the way muleys bound away by pushing off with all four feet at once, and landing the same way. That stiff-legged, spring-driven bounce has also given them the name of "jumping deer" or "jumpers." The pogo-stick-like movement contrasts sharply with the smooth-flowing gait of the whitetail.

When frightened, the mule deer is capable of attaining speeds up to 50 km (30 mi) an hour, horizontal leaps of 6 m (20 ft), and bounds that rise more than 2 m (6.5 ft) off the ground. These bounding jumps occur even when there is nothing to be jumped over.

The average mule deer buck within the Canadian Rockies is 140 to 180 cm (55 to 70 in) in length, 90 to 110 cm (35 to 43 in) at the shoulder, and weighs 90 to 115 kg (200 to 250 lb). A large buck may reach 250 kg (550 lb); does are considerably smaller.

This deer changes its coat twice a year. The summer coat is tawny or yellowish brown on the body, neck, and upperparts of the legs. The throat, inner ears, rump, and insides of the legs are white to creamy yellow. There may be one or two distinct throat patches. The underside of the body and the forehead are brown. In winter the coat is predominantly grayish, with long hair and a woolly undercoat.

Generally, only the bucks, like most members of the deer family, carry antlers, those producing large racks undergoing much nutritional stress. The growth process for the antlers begins in late spring, with the protective skin shed by August, and the antlers dropped by late winter.

The mule deer is a creature of open coniferous forests, aspen parklands, margins of meadows, streamside woodlands, and bushy situations. They move up and down the mountain slopes as the season dictates, climbing to treeline in summer and returning to the valley bottoms in late autumn. A recent study suggests that they are better at surviving extremes of cold than heat, possibly requiring more shelter to protect themselves from the heat of summer than from the cold of winter.

Mule deer are extremely catholic in their food selection. As they are known to dine on about 800 different plant species in the Rockies, generalization on diet is therefore difficult. In the spring they eat large quantities of grasses and grasslike plants. During the summer and autumn they eat many forbs, grasses, and leaves of aspen. Favorite winter forage includes twigs of deciduous shrubs and trees such as aspen, willow, red osier dogwood, serviceberry, sagebrush, and evergreens such as Douglas fir and western red cedar.

MULE DEER FAWN
LESS THAN ONE
HOUR OLD /
TOM J. ULRICH

MULE DEER FAWN
A FEW WEEKS OLD /
TOM J. ULRICH

MULE DEER FAWN
SIX MONTHS OLD /
TOM J. ULRICH

31

The breeding season, or rut, is the annual period of sexual excitement. As the days shorten in the autumn, antlers harden and the bucks become more active, competitive, and aggressive, with dominance scrimmages and other interactions becoming frequent. In one of the dominance acts, called rub-urination, a buck rubs his tarsal glands together and urinates on them. With the glands located on the inside of the hind leg just above the ankle, urine running down the buck's legs will carry their secretions to the ground, where the substance acts as a scent marker. A buck will also thrash shrubs and other vegetation as a signal to a competitor that he is ready to fight. Rubbing the forehead on vegetation produces an olfactory signal as well. Thus the antler-thrash and forehead-rub sequences provide both scent and visual clues to rivals of his presence. Other interactions among males include sparring and fighting. Sparring is ritualized: two bucks lower their heads and join antlers with forward pushes and head twisting, the match usually terminating when one participant moves away. Bucks use sparring to determine the relative size, strength, and status of an adversary. While jousting, they sometimes lock antlers, resulting in the death of both. Serious fights, generally involving bucks of similar size, occur when the reproductive stakes are high. Large bucks have noticeably swollen necks during this season, an indication of readiness to breed.

In order to determine the reproductive condition of a female, a buck smells the ground where a doe has urinated, retracting his upper lip, extending his muzzle, and turning his head from side to side. Scent from the urine passes to an organ in his nasal area, which will confirm the doe's reproductive status. After copulation, the buck turns his attention toward other does or toward maintaining his dominance. Most matings occur in November, which assures that fawns will be born in June, when the weather is warm and there is suffi-cient vegetation for a doe's milk production.

Although twins are common, a doe may have one to three fawns; one is most usual for the first pregnancy. At birth a fawn weighs about 3 kg (7 lb) and is immediately licked dry by its mother. The licking process enables the doe to identify her fawn and leaves it almost odorless and thus less vulnerable to an enemy. Within a few minutes the fawn can walk and is led away from the area where birth fluid saturated the ground and might attract a passing predator. In addition, the chestnut-colored fawn has rows of white dapples that serve as pro-tective camouflage. The dapples are gradually replaced by the winter coat. For about a month following birth, the fawn is hidden by its mother. She feeds some distance from her offspring so that her scent will not lead predators to the nursery. People sometimes find a bedded fawn and attempt to rescue what they assume is an orphan. Such fawns should not be removed or touched; the doe will return every few hours to nurse her young.

The natural predators of mule deer include wolves, cougars, coyotes, lynx, and grizzly and black bears. When protecting fawns, does may attack predators using their sharp front hoofs like spears. Unlike moose, they do not kick with their back legs.

Apart from the northern areas, where they are only occasionally present,

MULE DEER BUCK IN VELVET / TOM J. ULRICH

MULE DEER DOE / TOM J. ULRICH

you may expect to find mule deer throughout the Canadian Rockies except in the heaviest forest or the most open country. You are most likely to see them during the half-light of dawn and dusk.

Remember that it is illegal to feed deer and all other wild animals in the national and provincial parks. They receive little nourishment from junk food and may be unable to digest it. Deer fed in such a manner may become pests and in some situations dangerous, pawing at their provider with sharp front feet.

White-tailed Deer

Odocoileus virginianus

BJKCKNWY

DEER FAMILY

The most numerous and widespread big game animal of North America, white-tailed deer are found in Canada, northern South America, and all of the lower 48 states except California, Nevada, and Utah. There are more than two dozen subspecies of white-tailed deer on both continents, ranging from the tiny key deer in Florida to large, robust animals in western Canada.

A mature buck stands 90 to 105 cm (35 to 41 in) high at the shoulder, is about 190 cm (75 in) in length, and may weigh up to 135 kg (300 lb). Does are smaller. White-tailed deer have large, conspicuous ears, a naked nose pad, and long legs and hoofs, which adapt them for running. The upper part of the body is reddish brown in summer, changing to a grizzled grayish brown in winter. Although both black (melanistic) and white (albino) animals do occur, such cases are rare. The insides of the legs, underside of the body, and tail are white. The outside surface of the tail is brown, edged in white, set against a white

33

rump. When the animal is startled or alert, the tail is held erect and flared, an unmistakable feature of this mammal. The upturned tail, wagging from side-to-side, can be seen from a considerable distance and provides the inspiration for the common name of "whitetail" or "flagtail."

As with most members of the deer family, antlers are normally found only on bucks, but the occasional doe has small antlers too. The antlers are grown annually and differ from those of the mule deer in that the tines grow singly from a main beam rather than branching in paired beams and points. The number of tines on each antler does not indicate the age of the buck, as is popularly believed. The buck begins his antler growth in April, and the velvetlike skin that has covered the antlers during the growth period is rubbed off by mid-September, at which time a buck may become extremely aggressive and dangerous. In the Rockies, a whitetail drops his antlers in January.

Both sexes possess external glands on the forehead, hocks, and central toes of each foot that secrete chemical scents called pheromones. These scents identify individuals and are used by deer to mark their territories.

A whitetail's track is about 5 to 8 cm (2 to 3 in) in length, with a space of about 50 cm (20 in) between steps when the animal is walking. The hoof prints of a whitetail are not distinguishable from those of a mule deer.

WHITE-TAILED DEER BUCK / TOM J. ULRICH

WHITE-TAILED
DEER DOE /
TOM J. ULRICH

WHITE-TAILED DEER
BUCKS FIGHTING /
TOM J. ULRICH

WHITE-TAILED
DEER FAWN /
TOM J. ULRICH

The graceful white-tailed deer run in a smooth-flowing, airy gallop interspersed with great bounds or leaps. Although the gait seems effortless and drifting, it embodies great strength and power. They are mighty jumpers, reportedly able to cover more than 8 m (26 ft) in a running broad jump, and can easily sail over a 2 m (6.5 ft) fence. If not threatened, however, the deer would rather crawl under an obstacle than leap over it. They can run at a cruising speed of 50 km (30 mi) per hour for 4 to 6 km (2.5 to 4 mi).

Whitetails are most active in early morning and evening. Their senses of hearing and smell are acute and vision is excellent, especially in detecting movement. These high-strung, flighty creatures are cunning in their ability to remain hidden and protect themselves. During the hunting season they avoid hunters more effectively than many other big game animals.

Good deer habitat is characterized by forested areas of young, brushy stands with scattered openings. A combination of domestic crop areas, woodlots, and wetlands is ideal. Forest areas that have been logged or burnt, containing a lot of shrub and sapling-stage vegetation, are especially good for deer. Although whitetails spend most of their lives in the montane zone, it is not uncommon to see them in the subalpine and alpine during the summer.

Perhaps no other big game species in North America has been able to adjust to so many conditions, including many caused by human disturbance. These adaptable animals are known to dine on more than 1000 different plants and are not picky eaters, particularly when food is in short supply. In our area, white-tailed deer are primarily browsing animals, preferring buds, twigs, leaves, and fruit from plants such as aspen, chokecherry, red osier dogwood, saskatoon, and willow. They also eat grasses and a host of wildflowers, especially during the spring and early summer. Alfalfa, various grains, and other agricultural crops are part of their diet as well. They are especially adapted to a herbivorous lifestyle by having small, clipping, lower incisors, and large, grinding molars.

Most breeding activity among white-tailed deer occurs from early November into December. A buck marks his territory with scrapes on the ground and rubs on trees and shrubs. His neck becomes swollen with an increased blood supply and he becomes aggressive with other males, an indication of breeding readiness. He engages in mock or real battles with his rivals, and although no harem is established, a buck mates with as many does as he encounters.

The gestation period is approximately six and one-half months, with fawns being born in May and June. Although a doe's first breeding usually results in a single birth, twins are common in subsequent breedings, and even triplets are not uncommon, depending on the food supply. A newborn fawn weighs 2 to 3 kg (4 to 7 lb) and is able to walk on shaky legs within a few minutes of birth. Fawns have a reddish brown coat with spots that disappear when it grows its first winter coat.

Fawns move very little during the first few weeks, relying on camouflage and their nearly scentless condition to escape predators. Does may leave their young for hours at a time before returning to nurse and groom them.

The life expectancy of a whitetail is seldom more than 10 years in the wild; in captivity, deer are known to live as long as 20 years. Their natural predators include the wolf, coyote, bobcat, lynx, and cougar. In the northern reaches of the whitetail's range, severe winters with deep snow can cause widespread starvation by limiting food availability and reducing mobility. Severe winters may be the chief factor in controlling deer populations in those areas.

The range of white-tailed deer in the Canadian Rockies has fluctuated over the years, but for most of the region they are relative newcomers.

TWIN WHITE-TAILED DEER FAWNS / TOM J. ULRICH

WHITE-TAILED DEER DOE WITH FAWNS / TOM J. ULRICH

Although whitetails were present in fair numbers in the foothills at the time of the early explorers, their numbers dwindled to a low point near the turn of this century. They have since increased in number and aggressively expanded onto ranges as far north as the southern Yukon and Northwest Territories.

Fairly common in the open montane forests and foothills in the southern portion of the Canadian Rockies, whitetails are occasional to scarce in the northern parts. If you wish to see the elegant whitetail, remember that they are most active at dawn and again at sunset, when they venture to the edge of meadows to feed.

Moose
Alces alces

BJKCKNWY

DEER FAMILY

The largest member of the deer family, the moose is an animal of truly monstrous proportions. Although moose seem rather ungainly and ugly at first glance, they are really charmingly homely creatures. Adult males may be up to 3.1 m (10 ft) long, 1.9 m (6 ft) in height at the shoulder, and weigh about 475 kg (1050 lb). At a distance, the moose appears to be all black, especially if it is wet. A closer view, however, reveals that the dark color is only on the shoulders and sides. The back, head, and neck shade into a rusty brown with gray leg "stockings." It has long, slim legs and cloven hoofs up to 15 cm (6 in) long, which leave tracks that are generally larger and more pointed than those of wapiti. It has a ponderous head with a bulbous nose, long ears, humped shoulders, low-rumped, slender hindquarters, and a distinctive growth of skin and hair that hangs from its throat. That appendage, which serves no known purpose, is called a dewlap or "bell" and may be 25 cm (10 in) long, sometimes longer.

The ungainly looking moose takes its name from an Algonquin Indian word—*mongswa*—meaning "eater of twigs." In northern Europe and Asia, where it is also found, it is referred to as an elk, which has led to much confusion. In North America, the name elk is applied to wapiti. Such misnomers present a solid argument for the use of scientific names or the standardization of common names.

In North America, moose extend from British Columbia to Newfoundland and from Alaska, Yukon, and the Northwest Territories to Maine, Minnesota, and several states in the northwest, such as Montana, Washington, Idaho, Wyoming, northern Utah, and northwestern Colorado.

Males grow enormous racks of antlers, which first protrude from the skull in April and reach full size by September. Antlers are a form of bone, nourished during growth by a soft covering of skin and blood vessels known as "velvet." The velvet is removed by scraping the antlers against trees and bushes to reveal the white rack, which is soon stained a mahogany color. A new set is grown each year, as they are shed annually in December or January. As a male moose ages, the antler development becomes more massive, until the animal attains its peak physical condition and reaches the height of its sexual maturity in the seventh to tenth year. The antlers may extend 196 cm (77 in) between the widest tips, but more often span 120 to 150 cm (47 to 59 in). The heavy main beams broaden into large shovel-shaped palms, which are fringed with a number of spikes usually less than 25 cm (10 in) long. Large antlers may weigh between 25 and 35 kg (55 and 77 lb). It is through these immense racks that bulls win admittance to the gene pool.

Growing these racks requires about four months and great quantities of minerals and salts. Although thousands of sets of antlers are dropped each year, few are found, as those coveted storehouses of nutrients are soon recycled by rodents such as porcupines and mice.

A stilt-legged moose, with its large hoofs and dewclaws, is well suited to traveling through deep snow and wet areas. The cloven hoofs and dewclaws spread and support its enormous weight in any soft substrate. Moose run easily through snow and are powerful swimmers.

Moose run with their backs horizontal and steady, while each long leg moves up and down like a piston. When a step is taken, the leg is actually raised straight up, making it much easier to step out of deep snow or sucking mud. This gives them a gait on open ground that looks awkward to the point of being humorous. Those spindly legs, however, can carry a moose easily over fallen trees and through tangles of undergrowth. In spite of their huge size and

MOOSE BULL / TOM J. ULRICH

the thick forest cover they inhabit, moose can move with surprising stealth to escape danger.

The least social of the deer family, moose are normally silent and solitary except during the breeding season. For about a month starting in mid-September, bull moose become aggressive and advertise their presence with gruntlike calls or coughs. Though this is a challenge to other males, confrontations only occasionally result in battles. Most often, opposing bulls will paw the ground and thrash nearby shrubs with their antlers until one departs.

When two huge bulls fight, it is an awesome spectacle. They approach each other with rolling and swaying head motions. After repeatedly crashing into each other, along with colossal pushing and sparring matches, both bulls may be totally exhausted or wounded amidst many meters of torn-up ground, uprooted shrubs, and damaged trees. Young lovesick bulls that are driven off may wander a long distance searching for a mate. This sexually inspired wanderlust often results in young males showing up in towns, cities, and ranches far from their normal range during the autumn.

To attract his brides-to-be, the moose creates a wallow by pawing up a patch of ground, urinating in it, wallowing in it, then pawing it up some more. For some reason, cows find this irresistible, rolling in it over and over again.

Once ready to mate, the bull calls for a cow. When one within hearing range answers, the call is repeated until they get together. He will mate with as many cows as possible. Hunters, imitating the cow's call, can entice a bull within shooting distance.

Cows are much more vocal than the bulls during the rut. Their quavering moans have a coughing finish—*mooo agh*. Females may be aggressive at this time, indulging in frequent hoof-lashing battles, but the hostility is usually only toward other females, as they vie for the males' attentions.

The mating season is an exhausting and stressful time for the male. He may lose up to 20 percent of his body weight during the rut, and these high energy costs may render the dominant males more vulnerable to predators and other mortality factors.

Moose produce their young in May; a cow generally bears one calf or twins, but triplets are seen occasionally. The calves have unspotted, reddish brown coats that become darker within a few weeks. Although quite helpless for a time after birth, moose calves grow more rapidly than any other wild animal in the Rockies. Weighing about 11 to 15 kg (24 to 33 lb) at birth, a calf may gain 0.5 to 1 kg (1 to 2 lb) per day during the first month of life, and later in the summer, up to 2 kg (4 lb) per day. By the end of August they may weigh between 70 and 100 kg (155 and 220 lb). Within a week of birth they can swim and outrun a person.

The bond between cow and calf is extremely strong; unlike deer, the cow rarely leaves her young alone and it is prone to trail her almost everywhere. Sometimes a cow and her young seem to be permanent summer fixtures near a good marsh. If a human or predator is encountered, the cow lowers her head, lays back her ears, flares her nostrils, and bristles her shoulder hairs. If all that fails she may strike with her lethally sharp front hoofs. And unlike deer, moose kick with their hind feet as well.

Heretofore protective mothers become extremely aggressive toward their yearlings before giving birth to another calf. The bewildered young are chased off and attempts to return are vigorously repulsed. Yearlings are thus forced to become travelers and seek out new territory, which may lead to the use of newly created habitat resulting from forest fires or logging.

Wolves, cougars, grizzly bears, and black bears are the chief predators,

MOOSE BULL IN VELVET / TOM J. ULRICH

MOOSE BULL SHEDDING VELVET / TOM J. ULRICH

snatching calves and killing adult moose as well. Wolverines also prey on calves to some extent.

As an antipredator response, the calving season runs only a short four to five days. With many calves born in close sequence, predators can kill and consume fewer victims than might be possible were births staggered over a longer interval.

In some areas, moose are afflicted by a parasite called the meningeal worm, which attacks the meninges, or membranes, that sheath the brain. About the size of a human hair, the worm can destroy the tissues of the moose's central nervous system. Fortunately, this worm has not been found in the Canadian Rockies.

Although moose are associated with coniferous and mixed forests, they are also commonly seen in burned-over or logged areas interspersed with bogs, lakes, ponds, and streams. In the Rockies, an inadequate food supply is the major hazard faced by this animal. During the winter they live almost solely on shrubs and trees. Preferred winter browse may include willows, alder, birch, red osier dogwood, balsam fir, aspen, and poplar. When forage becomes scarce they straddle shrubs and small trees and ride down the stems to reach the tops. In addition, they may break off willow tops with their mandibles, and will also eat the bark from aspen and poplar trees when the snow is deep. Some winters, moose are subject to heavy tick infestations, and while attempting to get rid of the ticks, may rub themselves so vigorously that much of their hair is removed, exposing them to extreme cold.

In the Canadian Rockies, moose often have markedly different summer and winter ranges. They relish highly the lush green plants of early spring found most often on south-facing slopes where the snow melts first, and may

MOOSE COW WITH CALF / TOM J. ULRICH

even feed with their front knees on the ground in order to reach the first spears of new grass. Their summer diet includes grasses and aquatic plants. Frequenting shallow lakes and marshes, they feed on water lilies and other pond vegetation. Being quite at home in the water, moose are known to dive to a depth of 5 m (16 ft) in search of succulent roots on a lake or pond bottom. They also partly submerge in water during the summer to escape the torment of blood-sucking insects and to get relief from the heat. The daily food intake of these behemoths can exceed 18 to 27 kg (40 to 60 lb).

Moose are fairly common in the Canadian Rockies and foothills, and a good place to get a close-up view during the summer is at natural salt licks. Some of these areas are signed and others can be found by making inquiries of local naturalists.

It can be dangerous to approach these colossal animals too closely, particularly the helmeted and halberd-bedecked males during the tempestuous fall rut, or cows with young. Meeting a moose that is so large you have to look up to it is an awesome experience that you are not likely to forget.

Woodland Caribou   BJN
Rangifer tarandus   DEER FAMILY

The woodland caribou is the largest caribou found in Canada. Somewhat smaller than a wapiti but larger than a deer, an adult female averages some 135 kg (300 lb) and a male generally weighs about 180 kg (400 lb) but may reach as much as 225 kg (500 lb). A bull's pelage is usually a deep chocolate brown with white markings under the throat, belly, and rump. The hair is particularly long under the throat. Winter pelage is lighter in color, set off with a white mane. The female has similar markings, but is usually somewhat lighter in color overall.

Except in northern Labrador and Quebec, woodland caribou tend not to congregate in large aggregations of thousands of animals, a characteristic of northern mainland caribou herds. Unlike the barren-ground caribou, mountain-dwelling woodland caribou do not make long annual migrations. Elevational shifts of a few to a few dozen kilometers accomplish for them what long-distance migrations do for their barren-ground cousins—reduce predation and insect harassment and provide a variety of food.

Some woodland caribou in deep-snow areas may perform two complete elevational migrations each year, utilizing alpine meadows and upper subalpine forests throughout the summer and early autumn, and then moving to the forested valley bottoms during the late fall and early winter. About midwinter, when the snow is deeper and more compact, mountain woodland caribou move to the fringes of the subalpine forest, near treeline, where they feed on lichens that hang from trees, a dinner table they can reach only with the assistance of a deep layer of snow. With the approach of spring, the caribou move back to the valley floor to sample the first green growth of the season, following new growth as it moves up the mountain slope, until they eventually return to their alpine meadows for the summer. Woodland caribou are gregarious, usually moving in small bands and seldom traveling alone for extended periods of time.

The caribou is the only cervid in which both sexes usually have antlers. The antlers of females are small and simple in structure, although some can appear as miniatures of male antlers. The antlers of healthy adult males are immense compared to those of adult females, and much more complex in structure, with widely palmated lower lateral tines and palmated or fingerlike terminals on the massive main beam of each antler. Hierarchy within the herd depends largely on body size, which in turn usually relates to antler size. As the autumn rutting season approaches, males rub off the velvetlike skin covering their new antlers and are ready to fight for the right to mate. Bulls with the largest antlers have the best chance of controlling and breeding with the largest number of cows. Fortunately for the cows and calves, the antlers of most adult males fall off in the early winter, demoting them in the herd hierarchy. This loss of antlers after the rut is also accompanied by a loss of aggression toward other males and other caribou. As most cows retain their antlers until about

WOODLAND CARIBOU BULL / TOM J. ULRICH

calving time, they dominate and sometimes chase bulls away from feeding craters dug in the snow so they and their previous year's calves can feed first. Furthermore, sexual segregation—adult bulls wintering separately from cow/juvenile groups—helps to ensure the future of the herd, as the pregnant cows and youngsters can more successfully compete for food. If food becomes extremely hard to obtain during winter, however, the mothers will displace their young from the feeding craters.

Woodland caribou are well adapted to life in cold snowy regions. They

YOUNG WOODLAND CARIBOU / TOM J. ULRICH

WOODLAND CARIBOU BULLS FIGHTING / TOM J. ULRICH

have short, stocky bodies and a thick coat of long buoyant hair that insulates them and helps to preserve body heat. Their feet are especially well adapted for all seasons of the year. The large, elongated, concave hoofs splay out, snow-shoelike, to support the animals on snow or in muskeg, and function as efficient scoops to paw through snow in excess of 100 cm (40 in) deep in search of food. Where several animals have been feeding on the winter range, the landscape becomes pitted and begins to look something like the crater-marked surface of the moon. The broad, horny hoofs that protect the shrunken pads against the cold of winter are worn away by summer and are replaced by soft, enlarged, shock-absorbing pads.

The caribou's muzzle and teeth are ideal for cropping ground-dwelling vegetation. Although caribou eat grasses, sedges, horsetails, forbs, and mush-rooms, their primary source of food, especially in winter, is lichen, which require many years of growth to provide adequate forage for the animals. On the west slope of the Rockies in British Columbia, where deep snow precludes the digging of feeding craters, as much as 90 percent of the winter diet may consist of lichen from old trees that are typically festooned with these slow-growing plants.

An excellent sense of smell allows caribou to locate lichens under the snow. While working in the Tonquin Valley of Jasper National Park, the author had the opportunity to follow a small herd of caribou after the first deep snowfall of the autumn. Although terrestrial lichens made up less than 1 per-cent of the ground cover, all 20 of the feeding craters that he examined con-tained remnants of lichen.

Caribou run much like horses, with their necks stretched out straight. As the animals move, their hoofs produce an audible click that becomes especially noticeable when large numbers move together.

The full flush of the rut occurs during October. Gestation spans seven to eight months, so most calves are born in late May or early June. Reddish brown in color with a slight white wash, the youngsters are not spotted like deer fawns, but like most ungulates, the calves are mobile within hours of birth. Once the offspring can travel, small nursery bands are formed composed of calves and the maternal cows.

As a result of two breeding characteristics, caribou populations are unable to tolerate the high death rates that deer or moose populations can readily han-dle. First, most caribou cows do not breed until they are two and a half years old, compared with female white-tailed deer, which generally begin breeding as yearlings or even as fawns on exceptionally good range. Second, caribou cows normally bear only one calf a year, while moose and deer frequently produce twins and occasionally even triplets. The net result is that caribou populations usually have substantially lower reproductive rates than the other two species, thus rendering them unable to support the high levels of mortality that deer and moose sustain.

Recent studies with radio-collared caribou in the Willmore and Jasper areas indicate that wolves are an important predator. For a few years, caribou

WOODLAND CARIBOU THREESOME / TOM J. ULRICH

were killed at unsustainable rates by wolves, whose numbers are supported by other more numerous and perhaps less vulnerable prey species. Grizzly bears and cougars take a few caribou as well.

Their natural curiosity has also led to the demise of many of these animals. Hunters and photographers can often attract caribou to close range by slowly waving their arms or bobbing up and down.

Woodland caribou are unusual among the deer family in preferring relatively undisturbed areas; they are wilderness animals. Obviously this characteristic has important implications for management of their habitat. Growing human populations, railroads, highways, the loss of forest cover due to fires and logging, oil and gas exploration, as well as the clearing of land for farming, have severely reduced the numbers of woodland caribou in some parts of their range. In recent years, however, hunting restrictions and better fire control have allowed caribou to recover in some areas.

Unfortunately, woodland caribou in the Canadian Rockies appear to be in a precarious state with a rather bleak future. Although predators were controlled even in national parks up to 25 years ago, many human activities caused deer, moose, and wapiti populations to increase, which in turn permitted more predators to survive. Caribou are more vulnerable to wolf predation than wapiti or moose, when they occur in the same area, and they are particularly vulnerable when in poor physical condition. Caribou have been designated as a threatened species in Alberta and a vulnerable species in western Canada.

Most Canadians know caribou only as the animal on the back of the 25-cent coin. To see the rare and beautiful woodland caribou in the Canadian Rockies will take some effort and good luck. During the summer the best sites are above the treeline in Jasper National Park, particularly in alpine meadows along the Poboktan Trail above Maligne Lake, Mount Edith Cavell, Whistlers Tramway, or Tonquin Valley. During the winter, caribou are often seen on Medicine Lake, between Medicine and Maligne lakes, and occasionally south of Jasper townsite along the Icefields Parkway between Sunwapta Falls and Beauty Creek. In the spring, the most reliable viewing location is on the floodplain at the south end of Medicine Lake, where the caribou feed on horsetails. Other herds are present in northern British Columbia, particularly in Kwadacha Provincial Park and northward.

Pronghorn

Antilocapra americana   PRONGHORN FAMILY

The pronghorn is not a true antelope and has no near living relatives. It is a uniquely North American species, unlike the deer, moose, sheep, and bison, which all migrated from Asia.

The horns of pronghorn are unusual in several ways; they are not antlers, nor are they true permanent horns. They consist of two extensions of the skull covered by sheaths that are shed each fall, leaving stubs of horn about 7 to 10 cm (3 to 4 in) long. The sheath and horn cores are separated by a living layer of skin, with specialized hairs, that produces the next sheath. The blackish sheaths have a forward-projecting prong, while the tip hooks to the back. These features make the pronghorn unique in the animal kingdom. Mature bucks can grow horns 30 to 40 cm (12 to 16 in) long. On females, although they don't always have them, horns seldom grow longer than their ears.

Pronghorns are rusty brown to tan in color with white underparts, white patches on the rump, and black and white markings on the head and neck. Pronghorn bucks sport jaunty sideburns on the lower jaw and have darker faces than the females. The hairs on the vivid white rump patches, about 8 cm (3 in) long, flair out dramatically into a rosette shape when danger threatens, warning other nearby animals. They also emit a musty odor to warn animals that are downwind and out of sight of the potential danger. These dramatic warning systems enable pronghorn to send danger signals to others more than a kilometer away.

Pronghorns are the size of a small deer, with the shoulder height of a mature buck varying from 80 to 95 cm (31 to 37 in). They are about 135

PRONGHORN BUCK / TOM J. ULRICH

PRONGHORN DOE /
TOM J. ULRICH

PRONGHORN FAWN /
TOM J. ULRICH

PRONGHORN BUCK
WITH HAREM /
TOM J. ULRICH

49

cm (53 in) in length and weigh from 45 to 70 kg (100 to 155 lb). Mature females weigh less and are shorter.

Pronghorns have developed two important characteristics that have superbly adapted them to survive in the prairie environment: incredible speed and keen eyesight. Designed for speed, the pronghorn's legs are narrow, lean, and strong. Their leg bones are stronger than those of animals several times their size, enabling the legs to take tremendous pressure when traveling at high speed, and to avoid damage if they step into a hole while running. To supply all the oxygen required for their remarkable bursts of speed, the animals have much enlarged windpipes to nourish their oversized hearts and lungs. This uncrowned monarch of speed is the swiftest mammal in North America and is reputed to be second only to the cheetah in the world of speedsters. Unlike the cheetah, however, the pronghorn can maintain a cruising speed approaching 65 km (40 mi) an hour for a considerable period of time. Pronghorns, consequently, can outdistance most predators.

Although pronghorns can broad jump as far as 5 m (16 ft) as they race across their expansive habitat, they never developed the ability to jump very high. Even a meter-high fence is a barrier that they will scoot under rather than jump over.

The pronghorn's second vital characteristic for survival is exceptional eyesight. Their large eyes protrude from the skull, allowing peripheral vision forward as well as to the rear. In addition to the wide-angle view, the eyes are equal to strong binoculars in power. Reportedly, pronghorns can notice small moving objects up to 6 km (4 mi) away.

Unlike many groups of mammals, male and female pronghorns remain together all year. During the rut in September, pronghorns may be territorial or harem breeders. Does give birth after a gestation period of eight months, producing twins more commonly than single births, and occasionally even triplets. Tan in color with no spots, kids weigh 2 to 3 kg (4 to 7 lb) at birth. When danger threatens, they flatten their bodies to the ground and "freeze" while the doe tries to lead the enemy away from their hiding place.

Forbs constitute an important component of their diet, with browse critical during the winter, and grasses important as spring forage.

Pronghorns inhabit the plains, deserts, and foothills of North America. They are very rare in the foothills of the Canadian Rockies, but are occasionally seen near Police Outpost Provincial Park, east of Waterton Lakes National Park.

Bison   BNW
Bison bison   BOVID FAMILY

Bison, or buffalo as they are commonly but incorrectly called, play a prominent role in the history and folklore of North America. The term buffalo is applied more correctly to other types of wild oxen, such as the water buffalo, found in Asia and Africa. Bison first came to North America over the Bering land bridge during the early and middle Pleistocene, thriving amid the unbroken grasslands and northern forests. These shaggy animals roamed from Mexico to northern

Canada and from the Rocky Mountains to the Atlantic seaboard. Historically, six subspecies were recognized in North America.

Two living subspecies of bison remain on this continent—the plains or prairie bison *(Bison bison bison)* and the wood bison *(Bison bison athabascae)*. The former occupied the prairies of western Canada and the United States, numbering between an estimated 30 million and 75 million animals, while the latter ranged throughout the boreal forest of northwestern Canada and numbered approximately 170000. At one time, bison were the biggest aggregation of large mammals to tread anywhere on the earth.

When explorers first came to North America, the plains bison covered the prairies in such numbers it was impossible to believe that these great herds might ever disappear. Marveling at the numbers, they exhausted their supply of adjectives trying to describe the spectacle. Audubon, for example, said the roaring of the bulls was like the continuous roll of a hundred drums and could be heard for miles.

Yet this seemingly inexhaustible supply of bison was nearly exterminated between 1840 and 1885 through wanton destruction for hides and meat. During the peak of the slaughter in the 1870s, a railroad conductor reported that a man could walk for 160 km (100 mi) along the railway line without ever

PLAINS BISON BULL / TOM J. ULRICH

stepping off the carcasses of bison. Through such unbelievable and sadistic butchery, the plains bison were all but extinct by 1885.

The wood bison disappeared from most of its northern Canadian ranges during the same period that its plains cousins were being hunted to the brink of extinction. Only about 300 wood bison remained by 1894.

Conservation efforts, such as legislation in 1893 prohibiting the killing of any bison, the purchase and delivery for breeding purposes of 716 plains bison from Montana between 1907 and 1912, and a more recent wood bison recovery program, have led to an increase in numbers of both subspecies. The historic range of plains bison, however, is so modified that large, free-roaming populations will never be possible again.

Bison have a massive head, a short neck, and a high shoulder hump that gives the forequarters the appearance of being out of proportion to the hindquarters. They have rather short legs with large, rounded hoofs. Their tracks are similar to those of domestic cattle, as are their droppings. The heavy skull is triangular in shape and flattened in the front. The black horns of the males rise laterally from the side of the head and curve inward over the head. The curved horns of females are more slender. Horns of both sexes continue to grow and are never shed, true horns like this being characteristic of the bovid family.

The pelage of bison is composed of two layers—a woolly undercoat and an outer coat of long, coarse guard hairs. It is dark brown on the head, back, lower neck, shoulders, legs, and tail, and lighter brown elsewhere. There are two annual molts; pelage is considerably thicker and longer in winter. Albino bison, held in great reverence by the Plains Indians, are rare.

Wood and plains bison are closely related and therefore similar in appear-

PLAINS BISON BULL / TOM J. ULRICH

ance. Minor differences possessed by wood bison include a darker color, a more squarish hump with a gently sloping back contour, a larger size, a more massive skull, and longer horns. These and other differences are outlined in figure 6. The largest terrestrial mammal native to and extant in North America, wood bison bulls weigh nearly 1180 kg (2600 lb) and stand almost 2 m (6.5 ft) high at the shoulder. Cows of both subspecies are about 25 percent smaller than the males, although color and body configuration are similar.

Bison have a large repertoire of sounds including grunts, bleats, roars, snorts, foot stamping, and tooth grinding. Bulls may give roars and bellows during the rut that can be

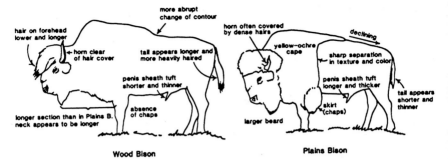

Figure 6. Basic pelage and morphological differences between a wood bison bull and plains bison bull, shown diagrammatically (taken from Reynolds, Glaholt, and Hawley, 1982).

audible for 5 km (3 mi) or more. They also use foot stamping and snorts during agonistic behavior. Calves bleat and give piglike grunts, while cows snort or grunt when searching for their calves.

All bison practice wallowing, rolling and thrashing on their sides in bowls or depressions about 4 m (13 ft) across and 30 to 50 cm (12 to 20 in) deep, which are created by their rolling activity. Wallowing in the dust or mud appears to give bison some protection from the torment of blood-seeking insects. Males also wallow during the rut.

Bison are less selective in what they eat than most other ungulates. They are primarily grazers, with grasses and sedges being the most important foods. During the summer they eat forbs and occasionally browse, but the latter appears to be of minor importance. Unlike some other North American ungulates who paw through snow with their feet, bison use their massive heads in a side-to-side swinging motion to sweep snow away from forage.

Bison are gregarious animals, matriarchal groups of cows, calves, and young bulls often numbering 10 to 20 animals. Such groups band together forming large herds, particularly during the mating season. Mature bulls seldom form groups of more than a few animals, and with increasing age, become less gregarious and are often solitary.

The rut and mating season generally occurs between July and October. After a gestation period of about nine and one-half months, a 14 to 18 kg (30 to 40 lb) calf is born; twins are rare. Although the calving period peaks during May and June, parturition can occur at any time of the year. Newborn calves are reddish to orange-brown in color, changing to a dark brown at about three months of age. Cow and calf pairs remain in close contact for several weeks, with maternal bonding and cohesion between the two being maintained throughout the year and sometimes longer.

Bison have an average life span of about 12 to 15 years in the wild, but in captivity there is a record of one living beyond 40 years. Wolves and grizzly bears are capable of killing bison, and major losses can result from accidental drowning by falling through thin ice or being trapped by spring floods. In addition, extreme climatic conditions, such as crusted or deep snow, can limit forage availability and contribute to further herd depletion.

Bison once roamed freely throughout the montane meadows and open woods on the eastern slopes of the Canadian Rockies. By the late 1880s they had been hunted to extinction throughout this area, and although the former multitudes of wild bison have vanished forever from the Canadian Rockies, there are nevertheless a number of good viewing opportunities. A herd of

PLAINS BISON COW WITH CALF / TOM J. ULRICH

WOOD BISON BULL / TOM J. ULRICH

plains bison can be seen in a paddock at Waterton Lakes National Park, and a number of small herds are kept on private ranches in the foothills. Bison may be removed from near the Banff townsite, but both subspecies can be compared at Elk Island National Park, a short distance east of Edmonton, Alberta. In northern British Columbia, a herd of a few hundred plains bison roam in the Pink Mountain area.

Bison can usually be watched with reasonable safety from a few hundred meters. Bulls are especially unpredictable during the rut, and cows with calves should be avoided. A pair of binoculars, a telephoto lens, and considerable respect for this magnificent wild animal should allow for safe viewing and good photographs.

To more fully understand the significance of bison to the indigenous people of the West, a visit to the Head-Smashed-In Buffalo Jump Interpretive Centre, 20 km (12 mi) northwest of Fort Macleod, Alberta, is highly recommended. That bison jump, among the largest and best preserved on the western plains, is designated as a World Heritage Site. The centre portrays the bison-hunting cultures from ancient times to the arrival of the Europeans.

Aggressive conservation efforts since the early part of this century are helping to ensure that these splendid mammals continue to survive as more than a symbol of a glorious past.

Mountain Goat

Oreamnos americanus

BJKCKNWY

BOVID FAMILY

Although it looks something like a goat and acts like one, the mountain goat is not a true goat. It is the New World's only representative of the rupicaprid, or goat-antelope tribe. Its nearest Old World relatives are the chamois *(Rupicapra rupicarpra)* of the European Alps, and the goral *(Nemorhaedus* sp.), serow *(Capricornis* sp.), and takin *(Budorcas taxicolor)* of Asia. Progenitors of the mountain goat are thought to have crossed to the New World via the Bering land bridge during the mid-Pleistocene Epoch. Finding safety in a bleak world of cold, rocky, and icy slopes in remote mountain heights, the goat prospered and evolved into its present form.

This superb cliff-hanger is well equipped for survival in the harsh climate of its chosen environment. A blanket of fine, thick wool, about 8 to 10 cm (3 to 4 in) long, covers virtually the whole body and acts like a thermal blanket. This in turn is covered by coarse, hollow guard hairs from 17 to 20 cm (7 to 8 in) long. Both these layers of pelage provide excellent insulation against the rigors of extreme cold. The woolly undercoat, even finer than cashmere, is visible in summer after the guard hairs and some wool have been shed. When the molt begins in May, the animals become extremely scraggly in appearance as the fleece sheds in patches from their heads, shoulders, legs, and lastly their rumps. The short, trim summer coat is replaced in October with the winter coat, producing the prominent double beard of long hair on the chin and throat, and "knickers" or chaps on the front legs.

The coat of this skillful mountaineer is white, sometimes with a yellowish wash. The lips, nostrils, horns, hoofs, and ebony eyes are the only dark parts of the animal. With their white pelage, they are difficult to see during the winter against their snow-dominated environment. In the summer, however, they often stand out against the blue sky or green foliage.

The mountain goat has a stocky, muscular build and a slight hump between the neck and shoulder blades. Other characteristics include a short neck, low-slung head, short legs, and a stubby tail. Mature billies are about 200 cm (80 in) long, 100 cm (40 in) tall at the shoulder, and weigh 90 kg (200 lb). Nannies are about 30 percent smaller.

Both sexes have short, stilettolike horns that curve backward to very sharp tips; they are not shed. Distinguishing male from female by their horns can be troublesome even for experienced observers at close range. The average length of male horns is 23 cm (9 in) with a basal circumference of 14 cm (6 in), while female horns average 21 cm (8 in) in length with a basal circumference of 11 cm (4 in). Horn growth can be as much as 7 to 10 cm (3 to 4 in) the first year, but much reduced in subsequent years. Horns of males have a slightly greater curvature than those of females, and curve from base to tip, compared to those of females, which curve backward near the tips. The spread between the tips of the horns is about the same as their length.

Mountain goats have crescent-shaped glands behind each horn, although they are only rudimentary on females. In males, these glands become more prominent during the breeding season and excrete an oily substance that is rubbed on vegetation by brushing the horns from side to side. This act serves to establish territories, intimidate rival males, and perhaps attract females.

MOUNTAIN GOAT BILLY PORTRAIT / TOM J. ULRICH

Visitors to the Canadian Rockies often confuse mountain goats with female bighorn sheep. Goats have white or off-white pelage; sheep are light brown with a white rump. The horns also provide an easy way to distinguish between them: goats have shiny, jet black, daggerlike horns, while those of sheep are an ochre brown. The male sheep grow large curled horns; the females' remain small.

Among big game animals of the Canadian Rockies, mountain goats, with their extraordinary climbing abilities, are the alpinists, moving up and down sheer cliff faces and leaping across 3 m (10 ft) chasms with ease. They are amazingly sure-footed because of the structure of their hoofs.

MOUNTAIN GOAT NANNY WITH TWINS / TOM J. ULRICH   MOUNTAIN GOAT IN SNOW / TOM J. ULRICH

Highly flexible, their hoofs are slightly convex with pliable pads extending beyond the horny outer shells, which provide greater traction by acting as spongy shock absorbers and suction cups. Their movements are generally deliberate, muscular, and stiff-legged.

Mountain goats have remarkable eyesight for detecting movement. Since all major predators roam below the realm of their normal habitat, goats' eyes actually point downward. Stalking a goat, therefore, is generally more successful from above.

Goats are seldom vocal. Adults grunt or bleat occasionally and the kids bleat.

Relatively sedentary with rather small home ranges, goats have no marked seasonal migrations. Except during the rut, the nannies, particularly those with kids at their sides, are dominant over the billies. Pregnant females establish resource territories in winter and aggressively chase out all other goats, big males included; by monopolizing the best resource territories, the nannies increase their kids' chances for survival. Within this matriarchal social order, the nannies and their offspring form small groups. Billies stay near the periphery of the resource territories as loners, or establish loose associations with other males, except during the mating season. When disturbed, a billy often reacts by stamping his forefeet and flicking out his tongue. He has a cantankerous temperament and is quick to defend his personal space against other herd members.

Mountain goats inhabit rugged terrain comprised of cliffs, crags, ledges, ridges, and talus slopes within the subalpine and alpine zone of the Canadian Rockies. The animals usually stay near almost inaccessible rocky terrain, where they can retreat from danger. During the summer, however, they may travel several kilometers through forest to indulge their strong craving for salt from natural mineral licks, many of which have a high concentration of sulfur, sodium, phosphorous, and soluble salts. This craving may indicate a mineral deficiency in their diet and the need for sulfur in amino acid production.

Mountain goats forage on talus slopes, ridge tops, alpine meadows, and timbered areas. In the winter they feed in areas of low snowfall or on south- or west-facing ledges exposed to fierce winds that blow the snow away, making their food more accessible. The distribution of goats is spotty because the combination of suitable forage, favorable topography, and good slope exposure is found in only a few places.

Snip feeders that rarely graze intensely at a particular spot, goats feed and loiter in bedding areas throughout most of the day, with feeding peaks at dawn and dusk. Grasses, sedges, and rushes are important in the summer diet, along with forbs such as lupine, bluebell, polemonium, and cinquefoil; shrubs like dwarf huckleberry, willow, and bearberry are minor components. Conifer utilization, particularly of Douglas fir and alpine fir, increases during the winter.

The breeding season extends from the middle of November through much of December. Only at this time of the year, when fresh snow reclaims the high country, do the males regularly associate with the females. The breeding males soil their beautiful white pelages at this time. Sitting on their haunches like dogs, they paw rutting pits with their powerful front legs, repeatedly throwing back snow and urine-soaked soil, which stains their bellies, flanks, and legs. During this time, they also mark clumps of vegetation with their horn glands.

Although fights are rare among billies, they can be vicious when they occur. The combatants do not clash head-on, as do sheep, but spin about side-by-side, thrusting at each other's rumps and bellies with their sharp, daggerlike horns. Although death from such gorings is infrequent, wounds and pierced flesh are not uncommon. Most confrontations, however, are harmless shams and bluffing matches. They may circle each other slowly, arching the crest of hair on their necks and backs to create an illusion of increased size during these broadside displays. At other times they may rush at each other, raking the air with their rapierlike horns, but stopping short of actual contact.

A courting male approaches a female in a low, crouching position with its head and neck extended. This humble, groveling approach is designed to appease the female and is in marked contrast to the broadside display used with males. Before mounting, the male often approaches the female from the rear and kicks her in the side or between her legs, testing her readiness to breed. If she is ready, the female will stand still after being kicked. The promiscuous billies wander from one nanny and kid cluster to the next perpetuating their kind.

About six months later, a pregnant nanny will withdraw from the herd and venture to an isolated rock outcrop to deliver a 3 kg (7 lb) kid. Single births are common, twins occasional, and triplets rare. The nanny-kid relationship is unusually close, with the nanny being both the protector and the teacher. Within hours the infant can climb and play games; within days it starts mouthing the kinds of plants eaten by its mother. The white-coated youngster nurses on bended front knees while its tiny tail wriggles back and forth. It can follow its mother over difficult terrain within a few days, but nannies stay close to their kids at all times, to ward off predators and aggressive males, and also to keep the youngsters away from cliff edges. In about a week the nanny grows restless and she and her kid rejoin the main herd, where the kids are able to associate with each other, playing games that help to develop muscles and coordination and aid in the establishment of a social order. Although essentially

MOUNTAIN GOAT NANNY WITH YEARLING KID / TOM J. ULRICH

MOUNTAIN GOAT KIDS PLAYING BUMP / TOM J. ULRICH

weaned at about one month, the kid associates with its nanny for about ten months. Winter losses are heavy and only about half of the precocious kids will welcome the spring, those that survive reaching sexual maturity at about two and one-half years of age, and full size at age four.

By choosing their home near the top of the world, goats escape the usual pressures from predators and competition with other ungulates. But they pay the price by living in a hostile environment at the upper edge of the life zone. Although cougars may take an adult and a golden eagle the occasional kid, predation is not a major mortality factor. Environmental factors such as avalanches, rock and mud slides, and lack of a good winter food supply are more significant causes of death.

Mountain goats are fairly common, but only in their chosen "top-of-the-world" habitat. The easiest places to observe goats are at natural licks. Some of the more accessible of these are along Highway 93 at Mount Wardle in Kootenay National Park, and in Jasper National Park at the Goat-and-Glacier Viewpoint on the Icefields Parkway, and at Disaster Point along Highway 16.

Bighorn Sheep
Ovis canadensis

BJKCKNWY

BOVID FAMILY

The wild sheep of North America are descendants of mammals that evolved some 2 to 3 million years ago during the Pleistocene Epoch. They reached North America during an interglacial period via the Bering land bridge that joined what is now Alaska and the Siberian portion of Russia. The Pleistocene was not an age of constant ice; there were several alternating cycles, when great glaciers advanced south from polar centers, followed by warm interglacial periods when the ice retreated. During this time many new types of animals evolved. The sheep that migrated from Asia to America, for example, became isolated in different ice-free areas, or refugia. Sheep in the Alaska and Yukon refugium evolved into thinhorn sheep, while those from the refugia south of the Columbia and Snake rivers in the United States evolved into bighorn sheep. These southern sheep then evolved into seven races and spread from the snowfields of the Canadian Rockies to below sea level in the desert of Death Valley, California, and from northern Mexico to the badlands and bluffs of the Missouri River.

Two races returned to Canada with the slow retreat of the glaciers. Rocky Mountain bighorns *(Ovis canadensis canadensis)* colonized the Rockies of Alberta and British Columbia, and the California bighorns *(Ovis canadensis californiana)* repopulated the arid mountains and river valleys of the Chilcotin and Oka-nagan regions in southwestern British Columbia. Although thinhorn and bighorn sheep of the Canadian Rockies could potentially interbreed, they have remained apart since their separation, with no overlapping of ranges.

Bighorn sheep are large, heavy-bodied animals with relatively long, slen-der legs. They have long narrow muzzles, short pointed ears, bobbed tails, and, unlike goats, beardless chins. Their eyes are large with yellowish amber irises.

Mature rams stand about 1 m (40 in) tall at the shoulder, are 170 cm (67 in) in length, and weigh about 130 to 150 kg (285 to 330 lb) in prime condition during the autumn. By spring these rams will weigh about 100 kg (220 lb). Adult ewes are decidedly smaller.

Bighorn sheep vary in color. Adults are a rich brown in fresh spring pelage, which pales gradually to grayish brown over the season. The pelage is composed of two layers, the outer coat consisting of guard hairs about 6 cm (2 in) in length, which are tipped with brown, and white at the base. Underneath is a short, thick, gray fleece, somewhat similar to the wool of domestic sheep. The chest, face, and legs are a darker chocolate brown, with the prominent rump patch, back of the legs, lower belly, and muzzle an ivory white.

During June and July the winter coat becomes matted and the sheep begin to shed their hair in patches. They look scruffy and bedraggled until their new coats grow in.

Both sexes have horns. Those of the rams are massive and curled, while those of the ewes are slender, slightly curved spikes. The horns of the ram—its crowning glory—curl back and down close to his head, with the tip of each horn projecting forward and outward just below the eye. These are true horns, growing from bony cores and never shed. Composed of keratin, similar to human hair and fingernails, the horns grow more rapidly when food is abundant. Horn growth is shut down during the rut, apparently because of hormones. This cyclic development results in distinct rings that can be used to age the animal. The tips of the horns on older males are often broken or splintered; this type of damage is called "brooming."

Although many visitors to the Canadian Rockies do not distinguish

BIGHORN SHEEP RAM / TOM J. ULRICH   BIGHORN SHEEP RAM WITH BROOMED HORN / TOM J. ULRICH

between female bighorns and mountain goats, the horns and coat colors are very different. The horns of female sheep are ochre brown, rough surfaced, and curved; goat horns are black, straighter, and more slender. Sheep are brown and white, while goats are completely white.

With front hoofs slightly larger than those behind, bighorns have unique, double-shelled, concave hoofs that separate into halves and spread over sharp rocks. Soft, roughened, cushionlike pads in the middle of these hoofs provide traction on slick surfaces.

The tracks of bighorn sheep resemble those of deer, but are generally more blocky or rectangular and more pinched in near the front. The tracks, however, can be confused. Sheep are capable of nimbly bounding up and down sheer mountain cliffs, being second only to mountain goats in the steepness of terrain they can conquer. The goat, in contrast, is more of a climber or walker, while the sheep is faster and bounds like a deer.

The voice of the bighorn ewe is the traditional guttural *"baa,"* and lambs make bleating sounds, both similar to those of domestic sheep. During the rut, rams frequently give a loud warning snort when preparing to fight, but generally, bighorns are rather silent when compared to their noisy domestic cousins.

Bighorns have eight sharp incisor teeth used for cutting off plants, and deep-rooted molars and premolars adapted for chewing this forage. All their teeth are gradually worn down by grit, which the sheep pick up while eating grasses and other low-growing plants, until feeding is impaired. Staple food items, which make up about 60 percent of their diet, include wheatgrasses, bluegrasses, fescues, and sedges. During the summer they also consume wildflowers such as peavine, lupine, pasture sage, and cinquefoil. Woody browse plants are generally avoided except during a time of scarcity.

Some biologists believe that the extraordinary eyesight bighorns have developed for detecting movement is equal to the human eye aided by powerful binoculars. Even slight movements and small objects can be detected over a long distance, so that on open mountain slopes predators cannot easily approach sheep without being seen. Since their vision is so highly developed, they have less dependence on their auditory and olfactory senses. Sheep can, however, pick up the scent of humans at a distance of more than 300 paces.

You may find beds made by bighorns when you hike the high country. Look for these beds on jutting points above cliffs or along ridge tops where the sheep have a good view of the surrounding country. They are made by the animals scraping at the dirt with their hoofs to make a slight hollow and are used repeatedly, so there is usually an accumulation of dung and hair.

Like thinhorn sheep, bighorns are intensely gregarious. Ewes, lambs, yearlings, and young rams form bands that stay together all year. During the summer, rams establish an order of hierarchy in which rank depends primarily on horn size, although dominance fights also involve body weight, quickness, and technique.

The resounding clash of horn against horn echoing through the mountain valleys as bighorn rams duel for dominance during the autumn rut is one of the

SIX-MONTH-OLD BIGHORN SHEEP LAMB / TOM J. ULRICH   BIGHORN SHEEP EWE WITH LAMB / TOM J. ULRICH

more exciting episodes of animal behavior. Most encounters are between rams of similar size. A confrontation begins with pushing and shoving and a display of horns by a subordinate to a dominant ram. This may be followed by kicks to the chest with a front leg, or a firm butt to the opponent's head. If the challenger's actions are tolerated, rank is transferred. If challenged, the two gladiators will battle when one ram feels it has an advantage and initiates action by rising on its hind legs and lunging toward its foe. The other reacts in a similar manner. At the last moment, heads rotate slightly and horns collide with a crack that can be heard for a kilometer. These head-to-head charges, at high speeds and with 130 kg (286 lb) or more of body weight for each ram, continue until one is exhausted or hurt and behaves in a subordinate manner. Sometimes one clash is enough; at other times they may fight for hours.

Surprisingly, few serious injuries result from such combat. To protect the brain and nervous system, the bighorn has evolved a double cranium. A few centimeters of spongy material between the two layers of skull and a thick facial hide give protection from the shock of such tremendous blows.

With the social order established, the dominant or alpha ram services most of the harem. As females come into estrus, they emit an estrogen; the male exhibits a "lip curl" as he lifts his nose to the wind and sniffs for the smell of the hormone. To prevent interference from other rams, a receptive ewe is then driven onto shear cliffs for mating. The dominant rams have a shorter life span than the other males. Weakened by constant attempts to defend females, which deplete fat reserves even before the ensuing winter's food scarcity, the rams are more likely to succumb to a predator or the rigors of winter.

The gestation period is about 180 days. Lambs are born in late spring when the expectant ewes leave the band to seek a sheltered ledge. Shortly after the lamb is born, the mother leads it back to the band for increased protection against predatory birds and mammals. Normally only one lamb is born, but twins occur occasionally.

The spunky youngsters play "follow-the-leader" and "king-of-the-castle" games that develop agility and strength. The lambs sometimes jump off the ground and twist their bodies in midair, a behavior called "gamboling," and occasionally adults join the lambs in this frivolous game just for the fun of it.

Bighorns are subject to a variety of mortality factors such as parasites, diseases, and predators, including humans. They are susceptible to a variety of lung pathogens, including viruses, bacteria, and parasites, which are sometimes responsible for major population reductions, and in certain cases have virtually wiped out some herds. Occasional accidental deaths result from falls, fighting, avalanches, and highway traffic. Wolves in the north and cougars in the south are the most effective predators, although others such as coyotes, bears, bobcats, and lynx may take the occasional newborn lamb or diseased or injured adult. The greatest threat of all, however, is the loss of habitat. Good quality winter habitat is lacking in some areas because of the invasion of tree cover. In other areas, humans and their livestock have permanently altered and overgrazed much of the bighorn's former range.

The habitats favored by bighorns include alpine meadows, grassy mountain slopes, and foothills in close proximity to rocky cliffs and ledges, which are used for escape cover. These animals require winter ranges with less than 1.5 m (5 ft) of annual snowfall because they cannot paw through deep snow to obtain forage. Some of the best ranges for sheep, such as the Cascade Valley in Banff National Park, are a result of forest fires and the snow-eating chinook winds.

Bighorn sheep are fairly common, year-round residents in the Canadian Rockies and can be found on the eastern slopes from Wapiti Pass southward and on the western slopes from Golden south. There are several good locations for observing them, particularly where they are protected within national and provincial parks. After generations of protection, these normally shy sheep are often easily approached. The following places offer good viewing opportunities:

Waterton—the townsite, Red Rock Canyon, Carthew Summit, and east of Crandell Lake on the grassy slopes above the Red Rock Canyon Highway (large bands are frequently present in the early spring).

Kootenay—Sinclair Canyon near Radium Hot Springs.

Banff—Vermilion Lakes area west of the Mount Norquay/Banff intersection, and Mount Bourgeau from the Sunshine parking lot.

Jasper—several good sites on Highway 16 east of Jasper, including the junction with the Maligne Road, Cold Sulphur Spring, Cinquefoil Bluff near Talbot Lake, and Disaster Point; Miette Hot Springs, Wilcox Pass, and the Mount Kitchener and Tangle Falls viewpoints on the Icefields Parkway.

No matter where you experience the majestic bighorn, it will be a lasting memory.

BIGHORN SHEEP
LAMB / TOM J. ULRICH

BIGHORN SHEEP
RAM WITH LIP CURL /
TOM J. ULRICH

BIGHORN SHEEP
RAMS IN SUBMISSIVE
POSE / TOM J. ULRICH

65

Thinhorn Sheep

Ovis dalli

BOVID FAMILY

Thinhorn sheep are perhaps the most beautiful of the native sheep in North America. Their long, slender horns flare widely away from the head and are usually pointed at the tips. Their bodies are somewhat smaller and more lightly built than bighorn sheep and they have a shorter, more pointed, face.

There are two distinctive races of thinhorn sheep in Canada. The northern race, Dall's sheep *(Ovis dalli dalli)*, has a somewhat ghostlike appearance with its striking, pure white coat. It inhabits the northwestern corner of British Columbia, the Mackenzie ranges of the Northwest Territories, and much of the Yukon and Alaska. Stone's sheep *(Ovis dalli stonei)*, the southern race, are quite different in color, and inhabit the southcentral Yukon and the northern Rockies of British Columbia. They have a blackish fawn back with white rump, belly, and leg trimmings, and a gray head and neck. Valerius Geist, a world expert on mountain sheep, describes Stone's sheep as being those in "evening dress." Although the color and pattern of the coat vary from range to range, the muzzle, rump, and back of the legs are always white. The "Fannin" or "saddle-backed" sheep, an intergrade where the two races merge, have a gray saddle patch over the back and tail but are otherwise white.

Mature thinhorn rams are almost 150 cm (60 in) in total length, about 94 cm (37 in) in height at the shoulder, and weigh about 90 kg (200 lb). Females are somewhat smaller, weighing about one-third less.

The ochre-colored horns of the males are anchored to the skull with two protective layers of bone over the brain. Weighing up to 10 kg (22 lb) and comprising 8 to 12 percent of body weight, rams' horns are weapons, shields, and indicators of rank. Horn growth is greatest in the summer and much reduced in the winter, a differential growth that produces annual rings and allows biologists to age the sheep. During the early years of a ram's life, the horn rings are several centimeters apart, but occur progressively closer with increased age. The horns reach about two-thirds of their length and 90 percent of their basal circumference by the fifth year. Ewes' horns are typically short and curved backwards.

Thinhorn sheep are highly gregarious. Rams persistently segregate themselves into exclusive bachelor bands away from the females and youngsters, except for the brief breeding season from mid-November to mid-December. Although this behavior exposes the rams to a greater risk of predation, it avoids competition with the females and their lambs. Leaving the better grazing areas to the females, who can then produce more and richer milk, helps to ensure healthy offspring, better able to survive the darkness and cold of the northern winter and to outrun predators.

Young rams leave the female society at about three years of age and attach themselves to a band of rams; the rams spend much of their time jousting with each other, bashing their heads together. This headbutting establishes the band's social organization and pecking order. Rams learn to judge each other's

DALL'S THINHORN
SHEEP RAM /
TOM J. ULRICH

DALL'S THINHORN
SHEEP EWE /
TOM J. ULRICH

DALL'S THINHORN
SHEEP RAM WITH LIP
CURL / TOM J. ULRICH

rank from their respective horn sizes, with a large ram reacting toward smaller ones by showing off his horns, although generally without aggression. The smaller sheep accepts its subservient status and either touches or rubs faces with the dominant animal. Young rams play female roles in the presence of

larger animals, resulting in homosexual behavior. Serious clashes to establish dominance are usually between rams of similar size. An attack is launched with a rearing start and ends with a powerful lunge and downward twist; the occasional battle may last most of a day. The loser, however, is only excluded from breeding; he may stay in the band as a

STONE'S THINHORN SHEEP RAM / TOM J. ULRICH

subordinate to the victorious ram. Losers are not expelled because many pairs of eyes are required to watch for predators, and there is increased safety in larger numbers.

In their own group, the older females tend their lambs and teach the younger ones the band's home range and the migration routes within it. The female band tends to maintain the same composition, while the rams rearrange themselves throughout the year.

Gestation lasts about 175 days, with lambing in May. Pregnant ewes leave the band and choose precipitous areas with escape cover from predators to have their young, which weigh between 3 and 4 kg (7 and 9 lb) at birth. Ewes usually give birth to a single, fuzzy, dark gray lamb, but twins are not uncommon. After the mother and offspring form a bond, they rejoin the band of females and young.

Nourished by rich milk from their mothers, lambs form groups and play chaotic games of follow-the-leader. Such scampering and prancing helps them to grow strong and agile, to prepare for the demands of a harsh winter environment, and to live within a rigid society. Although lambs start to nibble grass at about a week of age, they continue to nurse for about six months.

Nonhuman predators include wolves, bears, foxes, lynx, and wolverines, with wolves being the most effective. Golden eagles take some lambs as well, although deep, crusted snow, which makes it difficult or impossible to feed, is the greater danger. Mortality is high for the lambs—half of them may not make it through their first year—but is low between two and eight years of age. Although most sheep are killed by severe winters or predation by the age of 10 to 12 years, some live to be 15 to 17 years of age.

Thinhorn sheep are basically grazers of grasses and forbs, with staple foods including fescues, sedges, and horsetails. Mineral licks seem to be an important habitat requirement of these sheep, and may be a means of replenishing mineral reserves depleted during the winter, particularly organic sulfur, which is transformed by rumen bacteria and used in the maintenance of hair, horn, and connective tissue.

During the summer, thinhorn sheep inhabit alpine slopes and plateaus, moving higher with the green-up of succulent grasses and forbs. They descend to lower, drier ranges, usually with south or southwest aspects, during the winter. Rugged terrain is generally nearby to serve as escape routes from predators.

Most of the Stone's sheep populations in northern British Columbia are associated with winter ranges that receive snow-eating chinook winds. Many of the more dense populations, such as in the Muskwa River and Kechika River drainages, have access throughout the winter to subalpine grassland ranges, which have developed, for the most part, following forest fires. Lack of trees on these sites allows wind action and warmth from the sun to remove snow cover, making forage more available to the sheep. Sheep habitat and range in northern British Columbia have been extended and improved by prescribed and carefully controlled burning in certain areas.

Stone's sheep are fairly common north of the Peace River in northern British Columbia. The best chance of seeing them while driving along the Alaska Highway is in Stone Mountain Provincial Park near Summit Lake.

STONE'S THINHORN SHEEP EWE WITH LAMB / TOM J. ULRICH

Carnivores

(Order *Carnivora*)

Dogs (Family *Canidae*)
Bears (Family *Ursidae*)
Raccoons (Family *Procyonidae*)
Weasels (Family *Mustelidae*)
Cats (Family *Felidae*)

The order *Carnivora* includes mammals that are almost completely meat eaters to others that are omnivorous. Members of the cat family, for example, are almost exclusively meat eaters, while bears and raccoons may consume significant amounts of vegetation, fruit, nuts, and eggs. And not all flesh-eating mammals are included in the order. Shrews, for example, eat flesh but are classified as insectivores.

The major distinguishing characteristic for the order *Carnivora* is dentition. While the sharp incisors may be relatively small, the powerful canines are large, conical, and recurved. It is the carnassial teeth, however, that are the diagnostic feature. The carnassial teeth include the fourth upper premolar and the first lower molar, which work together in a shearing fashion to cut muscle fiber and tough tendons. In certain carnivores the molars behind the carnassials may be reduced in number. In addition to teeth that bite, crush, tear, and slice, carnivores are also equipped with powerful jaws for grasping their prey.

The senses of most carnivores are well developed, particularly those of smell, hearing, and eyesight. They also communicate in a variety of ways, including facial expressions, chemical signals, and vocalization.

Members of the order vary greatly in size. A least weasel, for example, weighs about 35 g (1.2 oz), while a male grizzly bear can weigh 385 kg (850 lb). Their behavior is also vastly different. Some live within a few hectares, while others travel great distances; some are solitary, while others form social hierarchies; some are arboreal, others live in burrows, while still others prefer aquatic habitats.

Carnivores originated about 60 million years ago. Now, on a worldwide basis, there are about 270 species within ten families in the *Carnivora* order. This diverse order is well represented in the Canadian Rockies, with 19 species in five families. Carnivores, however, are seldom numerous because meat eaters cannot outnumber their prey.

Coyote

BJKCKNWY

Canis latrans

DOG FAMILY

The coyote, or "barking dog," was originally native almost exclusively to the prairies and arid west. As settlers moved across the country, altering the landscape and doing away with wolves, a new ecological niche was opened for the coyote. With a dramatically expanded range, it is now the most widely distributed carnivore in the Western Hemisphere, thriving from the Pacific to Atlantic oceans and from the Arctic Circle south to Costa Rica.

Coyotes range in size between the red fox and the wolf. In the Canadian Rockies, adult males stand about 58 to 66 cm (23 to 26 in) at the shoulder and weigh from 11 to 18 kg (25 to 40 lb). The body length ranges from 110 to 146 cm (43 to 55 in) and the tail is 30 to 46 cm (12 to 18 in) long. The female is generally slightly smaller.

The coyote's long, grayish coat varies only slightly in tone. The back is darker than the sides and there is occasionally a darker band across the shoulders; the underparts are light. The backs of the ears and face are redder than the rest of the body, and the bushy tail, usually carried low near the legs, is darker toward the tip. Coyotes have long ears and a narrow, pointed muzzle housing long, slender canine teeth. They also have arresting yellow eyes, round in shape.

COYOTE IN WINTER / TOM J. ULRICH

Courtship of coyotes may occur for two or three months before successful copulation, with several eager suitors vying for a female before she ultimately chooses which male she will accept. A female will tolerate mounting attempts by the male and will flag her tail to one side when ready to mate; the coupling may last for up to 30 minutes. The female often gives precedence, if she has bred before, to her previous mate. The same pair may thus breed from year to year, but not necessarily for life.

In our area, coyotes mate from February to March. A litter of five to seven

COYOTE HOWLING / TOM J. ULRICH

COYOTE MOUSING / TOM J. ULRICH

pups is born in April or May, after a gestation period of 60 to 63 days. The pups are born in a concealed den consisting of one or more tunnels leading to a deep hole in the ground, often constructed from an enlarged rodent, fox, or badger hole. The female usually prepares alternative dens so the young can be moved to a safe place if humans or predators threaten.

Pups are born with short, yellow-brown fur. Their eyes open at about ten days. Both parents help feed the young. Early in their life, the male brings food to the female while she stays with the pups. Some of her partly digested food is regurgitated to feed the pups both during and after weaning. The pups venture out of the den to play at three weeks of age, and within two months the family unit abandons the den and travels together until fall. At that time the pups usually move out of the parents' territory, with individuals hunting alone or in pairs. Coyotes usually reach sexual maturity just prior to their second birthday.

The basic social unit is the male-female pair, but there is considerable variability, ranging from individuals to large groups or packs. Coyotes tend to be solitary when the major prey items are small rodents, and to form packs when large animals are available. They are also more social during the winter, when carrion is an important food resource.

The size of a coyote home range depends on several factors, but it generally covers from 13 to 26 km² (5 to 10 mi²). Coyotes mark their territory with urine, feces, and glandular scents; they also advertise their location with howling or yapping.

An opportunistic and cunning hunter that covers kilometer after kilometer searching for food, the coyote's favorite food is anything it can chew. Carrion of livestock and other large mammals is an important food source, especially in winter. It hunts small rodents, hares, ruffed grouse, and sometimes deer, especially the young when the snow is deep and crusted. It also relies heavily on birds, fish, amphibians, berries, and fruits, depending on availability. Coyotes stalk small prey using a stiff-legged stance and then pounce on the animal with all four feet.

In spite of our poisons, traps, guns, dogs, vehicles, and bounties, the adaptable and resourceful coyote has been able to survive and even increase in numbers. Its eerie, mournful cries can be heard throughout the Canadian Rockies, especially at dawn and dusk. Look for this "songdog" in grassy meadows and open woods.

Gray Wolf

Canis lupus

BJKCKNWY

DOG FAMILY

Wolves were originally distributed throughout virtually all of the major habitat types north of 20° north latitude, which runs through India and Mexico. In much of Asia and Europe, however, wolves have been persecuted for centuries and exterminated in many regions. In North America, wolves once ranged from Mexico to the High Arctic. As the continent was settled, their range was greatly restricted and numbers declined substantially. Today, wolves are extinct in the United States except for Alaska, northern Minnesota, Michigan, Wisconsin, and Rocky Mountain states such as Idaho and Montana. A highly contentious political debate is presently underway on the possibility of reintroducing wolves to Yellowstone National Park. In Canada, wolves still exist in 80 percent of their former range from British Columbia to Labrador and throughout most of the Northwest Territories and Yukon. There are no wolves in heavily populated areas of southern Canada, the maritime provinces, or Newfoundland. The total wolf population in North America is estimated at 60000 to 75000 animals.

Gray wolves, also called "timber wolves," are the largest wild members of the dog family. The average weight of a male wolf is about 45 kg (100 lb), but it can weigh up to 70 kg (155 lb). Their total length ranges from about 1.6 to 1.9 m (5 to 6 ft), including a tail from 40 to 54 cm (15 to 21 in) long, and they stand about 75 cm (30 in) at the shoulder. Females are usually about 10 percent smaller than males.

Wolves vary in color. A pack may contain animals that are black, grizzled gray-brown, to white, although the most usual color is dark gray with darker hairs sprinkled throughout the fur. Their ears are erect and their tail is bushy. Their four enormous canine teeth each measure more than 1 cm (0.5 in) across at the base.

There are a few ways to tell the difference between a gray wolf and a coyote, size being the most notable; a coyote is only half as big as a wolf. The wolf also has a broader face and less pointed muzzle. In addition, the coyote, when running, holds its tail low, while a wolf runs with its tail either horizontal or held up. Distinguishing between a wolf and a large dog, such as a German shepherd, can be more difficult. Here, tracks are an important clue. A wolf generally places its hind foot in the track left by its front foot and usually walks in a straight line. A dog's front and hind foot tracks do not overlap each other, and dogs tend to zigzag as they walk. Even when of similar size, the wolf has a larger head, longer and heavier paws, and a bushier tail.

Wolves are highly social animals, living in a pack or family group. A pack usually consists of six to ten animals including the dominant, or "alpha," male and female, pups of the current year, yearlings from the previous year, and subordinate adults. Pack size tends to be largest in winter. The alpha pair does most of the breeding, but recent research on captive animals and telemetry studies of wild wolves suggest that they may not be as monogamous as once thought. The alpha pair is in charge of the pack, raising the pups, selecting dens and rendezvous sites, capturing prey, and maintaining the territory.

Each pack of wolves establishes a territory that succeeding generations may occupy. Size of a territory varies greatly and is dependent on the kind and abundance of prey available. Territories covering 200 to 600 km^2 (80 to 230 mi^2) are not uncommon. The wolf density seldom exceeds one wolf per 25 km^2 (10 mi^2), and is generally much less.

Newly established wolf packs in Banff National Park have large territories, ranging between 1500 and 3000 km² (580 and 1160 mi²). The wolves there are also much more exploratory than previously thought.

Wolves scentmark the buffer zone around their territory with urine and feces, which function as "no trespassing" signs to possible intruders. Howling by a pack may also warn other packs to keep away from occupied territory. The edge of the territory includes a strip some 1 to 3 km (0.6 to 2.0 mi) wide, which may overlap that of neighboring packs. Generally, a pack encounters its neighbors only in this buffer zone. The inevitable result of such encounters are fights

GRAY WOLF / TOM J. ULRICH

BLACK PHASE OF THE GRAY WOLF / TOM J. ULRICH

75

that frequently cause serious injury or death to pack members, and because of this insecurity, wolves are reluctant to use the edges of their territories. Since the buffer zone is thus infrequently visited by wolves of any pack, prey species there will live longer and produce more surviving offspring than those in the midst of a pack's territory.

The wolf has one of the most sophisticated social orders of any mammal. Dominance and subordination, in which no member of a pack is equal to any other, are the keys to a pack's hierarchical organization and cohesiveness. The

GRAY WOLF PUPS / TOM J. ULRICH

social ladder is based on a pecking order or dominance hierarchy. A dominant wolf uses a repertoire of facial expressions and body gestures, standing with tail and ears erect, mane bristling, and legs stiff when meeting another wolf. The submissive animal drops its tail between its legs, draws back its lips and ears, and lowers its hind quarters. The subservient animal may also roll over on its back, sometimes urinating and whining.

A nonbreeding wolf may obtain dominance in one of two ways. It can stay with its natal pack and work its way up the hierarchy, or it can leave the pack and find a mate in an unoccupied territory in which to start its own pack. Disperser wolves may travel great distances in a short time. The recent establishment of wolf packs in northern Montana was likely a result of a dispersal of animals that moved silently south from the Canadian Rockies.

Wolves are sexually mature when two years old, but seldom breed until they are older. The dominant pair prevents subordinate adults from mating by physically harassing them. In the Canadian Rockies, mating usually occurs in February or March. In May, the female retires to a well-hidden den and gives birth to a litter of five to seven pups, occasionally more. At birth the pups are deaf and blind and weigh about 500 g (1 lb). Pups can see when two weeks old but cannot hear until after three weeks. Both parents, as well as other members of the pack, bring food to the young until they are about four months old and ready to participate in hunting.

Like most youngsters, wolf pups devote their early days to sleeping, playing, and eating. At first, the puppies' diet consists solely of mother's milk, but in short order, the young wolves supplement their milk diet with regurgitated meat brought back to the den by adults of the pack. The ravenous puppies, squeaking, begging, and wagging their tails, jump and nip at the adult's muzzle to trigger regurgitation. Within weeks, the pups graduate to eating unchewed meat.

Pups get attention, care, and food from the whole pack, not just their parents, the adults occasionally reverting to puppyhood and playing with the youngsters. These communal activities—feeding, playing, and howling—unite the pack.

In midsummer, the adults and pups abandon the den and the female carries the pups in her mouth to an area called the rendezvous site or nursery area, which is about the size of a football field. Here the pups explore every meter of the larger territory, as a sample of the free-roaming lifestyle that will characterize their adulthood. Their play shows a heightened intensity, and it is during this stage that they learn the lessons of dominance and submission. More than one rendezvous site may be used during the summer. The pack abandons the site in September or October, by which time the pups are almost full grown, able to follow the adults and start honing their hunting skills.

Gray wolves are carnivores, feeding on other animals. Their chief prey in the Canadian Rockies are large ungulates such as moose, deer, wapiti, and caribou, but their diet may also include beaver, hare, fish, birds, occasionally livestock, and some plant material. The Blackstone pack, just east of Jasper National Park, kills roughly 14 prey animals per wolf per year. With an average size of ten wolves, the pack killed 79 wapiti, 32 deer, 20 moose, 10 bighorn sheep, and 4 feral horses within a year. Wolves unquestionably have large appetites; 7 kg (15 lb) of meat at a sitting is a wolf's idea of a hearty meal.

Despite the large number of ungulates they kill, the lives of wolves are not easy. Prey animals are superbly adapted for escaping them, and it is estimated that only one out of ten attempts, on the average, ends with a kill.

Perhaps no sound in the wild is more hair-raising or spine-chilling than a wolf chorus on a crisp autumn evening. To many of us, the voice of the wolf epitomizes wilderness. But why do wolves howl? There seem to be several rea-

GRAY WOLF AT A MOOSE KILL / TOM J. ULRICH

sons for this form of communication. The cry of a lone wolf keeps the animal in touch with others in the pack, or with the den, and cohesion may be impossible without vocal communication to reassemble a dispersed pack. Wolves also howl to declare their territorial boundaries and to warn others that a territory is already occupied. Sometimes wolves may howl just to be sociable and to express happiness. In addition, the patterns of harmonies in each wolf's howl are quite distinct, so it is possible they may actually identify each other by howls. Even poor imitations of wolf howls by humans may elicit a response.

For centuries the wolf has been portrayed as a devil, the very essence of evil, and as a notorious bloodthirsty killer. Human fear, superstition, and outright hatred of the animal resulted in sustained efforts to exterminate wolves. European settlers in North America eradicated wolves from more than 50 percent of their former range, and even in some of our national parks they were poisoned, hunted, and trapped out of existence. But there has been a remarkable change of attitude toward this ultimate carnivore in recent years, from hate to admiration and almost worship. Attitudes have changed; mass persecution has ended; and real efforts are being made to manage and preserve these spectacular animals. Much of this about-face is based on new understandings, obtained from recent research, that demonstrated the intelligence of wolves, their caring and cooperative family structure, and the complexity of their lives. Wolves display many human characteristics, such as pairbonding, ability to train their young, and willingness to share with one another. The image of the wolf has changed from a cunning seducer of little girls with red hoods and a devourer of people, to the symbol of all that is valued in wilderness. Despite some remaining antiwolf sentiments, it is now allowed to occupy its rightful place in the ecosystem.

While wolves are featured in several fairy tales, such as *Little Red Riding Hood* and *Peter and the Wolf*, there are also biological fairy tales about wolves. In the past, much has been made of the "balance of nature." Many people believed that wolves killed only the sick, weak, or aged, and that the numbers of predator and prey remained fairly constant. It is clear now that under favorable circumstances wolves kill many young ungulates and even adults in prime condition. They kill because they have to survive, but compelling evidence indicates that wolves can play a key role in depressing the numbers of ungulates in certain areas, even to the point of raising the mortality rate above the rate of replacement. In Alaska, for example, moose calves and yearlings and caribou increased two- to four-fold where wolves were controlled. In the central and northern portion of the Canadian Rockies, the small, endangered population of woodland caribou are easier prey than deer, moose, or wapiti, so they tend to be killed by wolves. If caribou are to be given a reasonable chance to stage a comeback, reduction of the wolf population associated with the caribou herds may be essential. But the ethics of removing one animal to favor another are complex and controversial—one of the more difficult aspects of a wildlife biologist's job.

Red Fox

Vulpes vulpes

A member of the *Canidae* family, the red fox is the most common fox species in North America. The smallest native member of its family in the Canadian Rockies, the red fox weighs 3 to 7 kg (7 to 15 lb), stands about 35 cm (14 in) at the shoulder, and is about 1 m (40 in) in length, excluding the tail. They may appear to be much larger because of their thick, full coat of fur. The 30 to 45 cm (12 to 18 in) blackish or buff-colored tail is bushy, almost cylindrical in shape, and is characteristically tipped with white, which distinguishes the red fox from any other native fox in North America. The tail is used for balance, scent communication, visual displays, and for keeping the face warm while sleeping. Red foxes are trim and long-legged, with a long snout, large, erect ears, and yellow to brown eyes with narrow pupils.

The typical red fox varies in color from russet red to sandy blonde, being darkest on the lower back. Underparts are usually white, and the legs, feet, and back of the ears are generally black. Unfortunately, the name red fox does not reflect the other color phases that occur, including the black, silver, and cross foxes. The black fox is black all over; the silver fox has black hair tipped with white; and the cross fox bears a dark stripe that extends from the head down the center of the back, with another stripe that crosses from shoulder to shoulder. Most silver foxes are black foxes during summer and only turn silver when the guard hairs grow into the winter coat. All three color phases may occur in a single litter.

The red fox has a great ability to adapt to new and human-created environments. For that reason, it can be found almost anywhere including farmland,

RED FOX / TOM J. ULRICH

beaches, prairies, woodlands, and both alpine and arctic tundra. Its populations appear to do best, however, along the edge of forests, tilled fields, and near marshes.

Red foxes maintain well-defined family territories that overlap only occasionally. Like dogs, they mark their territory by urinating on rocks, grasses, and other low objects to warn off strangers. If that does not work, resident foxes defend their territory with threat displays and chases. Habitat quality and food availability influence the size of their home ranges. In diverse habitat, red foxes may live in an area less than 1 km² (0.4 mi²) in size. In less diverse habitat, as much as 5 to 8 km² (2 to 3 mi²) may be required to fulfil their needs.

Red foxes are crepuscular; that is, peak activity generally occurs near sunset and sunrise, although daylight activity increases during winter when food becomes more scarce.

Well-developed senses of hearing, sight, and smell make this intelligent animal an efficient and lethal predator with a variety of hunting styles for capturing different types of prey. When hunting mice, a red fox stalks within pouncing distance, lunges up to 4 m (13 ft), and tries to pin its quarry with the front feet. In contrast, hares and rabbits are generally stalked, then run down in a hell-bent-for-leather chase. Though a member of the dog family, the red fox hunts more like a cat than a dog. In fact, because of the type of predator it has evolved to be, the red fox shows many catlike characteristics in its physical appearance and behavior. Both foxes and cats have long, sensitive whiskers;

RED FOX PORTRAIT / TOM J. ULRICH

thin, daggerlike canine teeth; and vertically slit pupils. They also share a highly developed sense of balance, lateral threat displays—arched back with fur standing erect over the body and tail—and similar hunting patterns.

The dog and the vixen, as the male and female are called, begin traveling together during the coldest part of the winter and soon become preoccupied with courtship. After mating in late January to mid-March, the pair will start looking for a den, often choosing an old badger or porcupine burrow that they rearrange to their taste. Since a fox is not well equipped to dig, its dens are often in loose soil. The dens used for birthing generally face

RED FOX KIT / TOM J. ULRICH

south and have several entrances. For security reasons, more than one den is generally established.

After a gestation period of about 53 days, from one to ten young are born, the average being five. The kits or whelps, as they are sometimes called, are 15 to 20 cm (6 to 8 in) long and weigh 100 to 110 g (4 oz) at birth. The kits' eyes open when they are about nine days old, and they are weaned at about five weeks of age. Both parents hunt in order to feed the young. After being weaned, the kits stay close to the den entrance and rush inside at the first sign of danger. At about six weeks of age, the kits begin to accompany their parents on hunting expeditions, and by autumn, the family splits up and the kits leave the home den to fend for themselves. A female offspring may stay on the family territory and assist the parents in raising the next litter the following spring.

RED FOX KITS / TOM J. ULRICH

RED FOX KITS PLAYING / TOM J. ULRICH

The red fox has many enemies, particularly the coyote. Trappers have a saying that "when the coyote moves in, the red fox moves out." Wolves, lynx, and humans are also predators. In addition, the red fox is susceptible to rabies and is a significant carrier of that disease in some areas.

Red foxes are occasional year-round residents and are slowly expanding their range throughout the Canadian Rockies. Try not to miss the joy of seeing this tricolor beauty—red coat, black bootlets, and white vest. Look for them on grassy meadows and open woods.

Black Bear

Ursus americanus

BJKCKNWY

BEAR FAMILY

Despite their name, black bears vary in color from almost white to black. The usual color within the Canadian Rockies is a glossy black, except for a tan patch across the nose, and some animals have white markings of various shapes and sizes on their chests. Chocolate brown and cinnamon color phases occur in the Canadian Rockies, while white and cream-colored animals are found along the northern Pacific coast. It is possible to have marked color differences even within the same litter.

Widely distributed in North America, black bears are bulky, thickset, and rounded, with short, sturdy legs. In the Canadian Rockies, adult males average about 135 to 175 cm (53 to 69 in) in length, stand 100 to 120 cm (39 to 47 in) at the shoulder, and weigh 100 to 150 kg (220 to 330 lb). Females of a similar age are generally considerably smaller. Other characteristics include a moderate-sized head, small eyes, rounded ears, a short tail, and a tapered muzzle with large nostrils. The deep pockets between the lips and the gums allow their lips to be moved with amazing dexterity, which greatly assists them in deftly removing berries and fruit from branches.

A grizzly can be distinguished from a black bear by its massive head; small, wide-set conical ears; dished or concave face; large hump of powerful muscle over the front shoulders; and claws that protrude well beyond the front of the paws (figure 7). The foreclaws are heavier, longer, broader, and straighter than those of its black bear cousin.

Black bears walk on the soles of their feet, like a person, with the entire bottom part of the hind foot touching the ground. The toes on each foot are equipped with five curved, nonretractable claws that are used for digging, tearing open logs, and climbing trees.

These bears are able to run surprisingly fast, up to 55 km (35 mi) an hour over short distances. They are strong swimmers and also quite adept at climbing trees. Although their eyesight may be relatively poor, some research suggests that they can detect color, which may be advantageous to them in selecting ripe fruits. These shy animals also possess keen smell and hearing, senses that are useful in avoiding humans.

Good black bear habitat is characterized by extensive, heavily forested areas and dense bush. Black bears tend to wander considerable distances, with

BLACK BEAR / TOM J. ULRICH

GRIZZLY BEAR

Hump

Rump lower than shoulders

Dish-shaped profile

Ruff of long fur

Claws longer and less curved

Claws longer

Toes closer together and less arced

BLACK BEAR

Hump absent

Rump higher than shoulders

Straight profile

Ruff absent

Claws shorter and more curved

Claws shorter

Toes more separated and more arced

Figure 7. Characteristics of grizzly and black bears.

some adult males having lifetime ranges of 1300 to 1600 km² (500 to 620 mi²). The home ranges of females are usually quite restricted, perhaps 40 km² (15 mi²) or less. Bears will signal their presence in an area by repeatedly clawing, biting, and rubbing trees along trails and other areas they frequent.

Black bears eat both plant and animal matter, changing their diet with seasonal food availability. When first emerging from the winter den, they feed primarily on green, herbaceous vegetation and occasionally on carrion and small mammals. During the summer and fall, bears feed extensively on green vegetation and on wild fruit and berries such as blueberries, soapberries, strawberries, elderberries, and saskatoons. Insects such as ants and grasshoppers, along with their eggs and larvae, are highly prized. Bears also eat the inner bark of shrubs and trees, which are high in protein and sugar. Other foods may include livestock, beehives, garbage, and cultivated crops. Bears do not respect the "please-don't-pick-the-wildflowers" rule common to most parks; the author

BLACK BEAR CUB / TOM J. ULRICH

BLACK BEAR FEEDING / TOM J. ULRICH

once watched a bear feed on dandelions for more than 30 minutes. At the end of lunch, its muzzle was stained bright yellow from the flowers it had eaten.

Plentiful berry crops and good foraging conditions in the summer and autumn are essential for the survival of bears. Living off an energy-rich layer of fat during the winter, they may lose up to 30 percent of their pre-denning weight, so the accumulation of fat reserves before denning is critical. Consuming as many as 20000 calories a day results in dramatic weight gains as they prepare for their Rip-Van-Winkle-like sleep. They do not defecate, urinate, drink, or feed during the denning period, and the intestinal tract becomes blocked with a fecal plug until the bears emerge in the spring.

Apart from the strong bond between the female and cubs, black bears are solitary animals except during the breeding season. At that time, the female wanders throughout her territory, leaving scent trails, which the males follow. When the sexes meet, the male chases the female until they mate. Both males and females may breed with several mates, with males fighting fiercely while competing for females. The mating season extends from June to early July, with the cubs born the following January or February. Although the normal litter size is two, three and four cubs are not uncommon. Born in the winter den, the young are hairless and sightless at birth, and inordinately small, being about 20 cm (8 in) in length and weighing only 225 g (8 oz). The cubs grow rapidly, however, and emerge from the den in April. The mother cares diligently for her offspring and appears to teach them through a variety of actions and sounds, schooling and protecting them for approximately 16 months. The cubs usually sleep with mom during their first full winter of life and then, during the following spring, they are chased off so she can breed again. Siblings sometimes stay together after their mother leaves them.

Few animals are a threat to a full-grown black bear, although grizzlies, wolves, cougars, and especially humans are counted among its enemies.

Black bears are fairly common in the montane zone of the Canadian Rockies and may extend to almost any habitat below treeline. They are often seen around campsites, beside roads, and along trails at any hour of the day, and except for the roadside panhandlers clownishly looking for handouts, they are generally wary creatures. Intelligent and adaptive, bears are also unpredictable, especially when cubs or food are present, and should be observed from a distance. They can be extremely aggressive after they lose their fear of humans.

Grizzly Bear

Ursus arctos

BJKCKNWY

BEAR FAMILY

The largest and most powerful carnivore in the Rockies, the grizzly bear derives its name from the lighter-tipped hairs that give its coat a grizzled look, especially on the face and shoulders. For the same reason, it is often called a "silvertip."

At the time of European settlement, the grizzly roamed from the Arctic to Mexico and from the West Coast to the center of the continent. Hundreds of thousands of these bruins inhabited the prairies, river bottoms, and mountains.

With settlement, however, the grizzly gradually disappeared, except from the Rocky Mountains, Alaska, and northern Canada.

There is much individual variation among grizzlies. At one time, some biologists recognized 87 different species in North America alone. They have now been lumped as a single species, but one that shows considerable variation over its range.

Adult male grizzlies weigh from 150 to 385 kg (330 to 850 lb), are 1.8 to 2.2 m (6 to 7 ft) in length from head to tail, and stand 0.9 to 1.1 m (3 to 3.5 ft) at the shoulder. Younger animals and females may be considerably smaller.

The pelage of grizzly bears consists of an underfur of fine hairs overlaid with coarse guard hairs, often complemented by a full, thick mane of guard hairs from the base of the skull to the shoulders. Their coats of many colors are extremely variable, ranging from creamy yellow to almost black, although the dark brown color phase with white-tipped hairs around the face and over the shoulders is dominant in the Canadian Rockies. The thick underfur is rubbed off during the late spring and early summer and replaced with a thin coat for the warm weather. By October the bears are once again resplendent in their long, glossy winter coats.

The grizzly bear has a mixed bag of senses. Its eyesight may be poor; its hearing is good; and its sense of smell, used to detect rotting carcasses and human garbage from a distance of several kilometers, is extraordinary.

This bear is a swift runner over short distances, a good swimmer, and has prodigious strength. It can kill most large ungulates with a single blow and can drag an animal as large as a bull wapiti up a mountainside.

Grizzly bears are elusive, secretive, and partly nocturnal. They are active during the early morning and evening and sometimes throughout the day.

Although they are confined to dens during the winter, males and females without cubs are free spirits during the summer, when home ranges may span 3900 km^2 (1500 mi^2).

Grizzly bears, like humans, are omnivorous, eating both plants and animals. Their teeth include the molars of a herbivore and the canines of a carnivore. Recent research indicates that grizzlies are extremely sensitive to plant phenology and have sophisticated feeding strategies, with the largest portion of their diet composed of green vegetation, roots, and berries during the appropriate season. In the Canadian Rockies, important spring food plants include sweetvetches, horsetail, various grasses and sedges, cow parsnips, and mountain sorrel. Grizzlies also dig up and consume tubers of the glacier lily and spring beauty, as well as other bulbs. In the summer and early fall, the fruits of elderberry, bearberry, highbush cranberry, crowberry, serviceberry, soapberry, and several kinds of blueberries attract their attention. They also tear up great furrows in the vegetation to find mice, ground squirrels, and marmots in their burrows. In some areas, they consume large quantities of insects, fungi, and fish.

Grizzlies readily eat carrion, and occasionally kill deer, moose, wapiti, black bears, or even grizzly bear cubs. When they emerge from their dens in the spring, winter-killed or weakened animals may become an important part of their diet. After eating its fill, a grizzly will cover the carcass of a large ungulate with branches and snow or dirt, returning to the site of the kill until the carcass is completely consumed. At other times, the bears concentrate their attention on young animals, and will occasionally kill domestic livestock on ranches in the foothills.

Bears feed vigorously to regain the weight lost during the previous winter and to store fat for the coming winter. Their rich fat has about 7700 calories per kg (3500 calories per lb).

Humankind is the only enemy of these great carnivores, with poaching, hunting, and especially destruction of wilderness habitat being responsible for the demise of the grizzly in some regions.

Preferring open country, grizzly bears are found in the foothills, montane, subalpine, and alpine zones of the Canadian Rockies. Although it was once thought that nearly all grizzlies spent the summer in high terrain, recent studies indicate that some grizzlies spend the entire year, except for denning, in the valley bottoms. Some of the boars (males), in particular, are wide ranging and can be expected to appear almost anywhere their food is abundant. Some females with cubs prefer isolated subalpine or alpine cirques for raising their families.

Winter denning sites are usually located on eastern or northern slopes, at or near treeline, with a typical den consisting of a small opening, a short passageway, and a sleeping chamber not much larger than the bear itself. The chamber is often lined with conifer boughs and grasses. Although considered not to be true hibernators because of their high body temperature, bears spend their winter dormancy in lethargic slumber.

Grizzlies reach breeding maturity by the age of six or seven years. A male

GRIZZLY BEAR / TOM J. ULRICH

may confine a female on a mountain top for up to 15 days, isolating her from other males until she comes into heat and is bred, sometime in June or July. Copulation lasts from 5 to 60 minutes and may be repeated several times over a few days. These bears are definitely promiscuous, with both sexes having several partners. The mating success of the male depends on defending a territory that overlaps those of several females.

The embryo does not begin to develop in the female until fall, when she dens up for winter. Females have little to do with males until their next estrus,

GRIZZLY BEAR AT KILL / TOM J. ULRICH

GRIZZLY BEAR SOW WITH CUBS / TOM J. ULRICH

three or four years hence, because the boars may kill cubs or yearlings if given the opportunity.

Generally, two cubs are born in January, although a litter may range from one to four. At birth cubs weigh only 340 to 680 g (12 to 24 oz) and measure 25 cm (10 in) from nose to tail. Coats of silky, dark fur cover their bodies, and their eyes remain closed for several weeks. Tiny at birth, cubs grow rapidly, weighing about 10 kg (22 lb) by the time they emerge from the den in April or May.

Although they are weaned at about five months, mom sees her cubs through their second year and stands ready to savagely defend them, whether they are newborns or 50 kg (110 lb) budding giants. Sows are infamous for their possessive nature toward their cubs, and most serious injuries to humans result from females defending their young.

The cubs are full of unbridled energy, galloping, running, jumping, rolling about, pouncing on each other, and wrestling. Such rough-and-tumble action hones their physical skills and lets certain cubs become dominant over others.

Grizzly bears have a very low reproductive rate. A female is often more than five years old before she breeds for the first time, and she will produce only one to four cubs every three or four years. For this reason, management of grizzly bear populations on the conservative side is critical to their well-being.

While visitors to the Canadian Rockies may have both a great fascination for and irrational fear of the continent's most powerful creature, the grizzly bear is often the animal they most want to see. Visitors should realize that bear attacks are extremely rare occurrences, the injury rate from grizzlies being 1 per 1 million visitors. Even in the backcountry, the rate is 1 injury per 5000 to 70000 backcountry days. In comparison, car accidents, falls, bee stings, and lightning strikes are far more dangerous than bears. Generally, the bears are dangerous only when surprised, cornered, wounded, or with cubs. As a precaution, be knowledgeable about bears and their signs, respect them, be wary of them, avoid them if you can, but don't worry unnecessarily about them. Welcome the opportunity to see one of nature's magnificent creatures, perhaps just around the next corner of the trail or curve in the highway! It is a thrill to see a bear in a natural setting. Even finding footprints or discovering a scat can be exciting since the grizzly epitomizes everything that we know as wild. Readers interested in the causes of and methods for avoiding bear attacks are referred to the excellent book on that subject by Herrero (1985). The "griz" is occasional throughout the Canadian Rockies, and may be encountered in any environment from low elevation to high above treeline.

Raccoon

JW

Procyon lotor

RACCOON FAMILY

Native to North America, raccoons are found commonly throughout the United States, southern Canada, and as far south as Central America and the West Indies. Their natural haunts are open forests, stream edges, and coastal marshes. Although still few in number, raccoons are expanding their sphere into the foothills of the Canadian Rockies.

The most notable physical characteristics of the raccoon are its conspicuous black mask on a whitish face and a bushy tail with as many as four to seven black rings. The general body color is gray to black on the dorsal side, depending on the relative number of black- and white-tipped guard hairs, and paler on the underside. The fine underfur is uniformly gray or brownish. Adult males are 80 to 95 cm (31 to 37 in) in total length and weigh from 5 to 16 kg (11 to 35 lb) or more. The ringed tail comprises about one-third of its total length.

Raccoons' toes are not webbed and can be opened wide, and like monkeys, their forepaws can be used with great skill. These well-developed grasping "hands" allow dexterous manipulation of objects and a tenacious grip.

Although raccoons are associated with wooded areas, they neither hunt their prey in trees nor feed on bark and twigs. Trees offer, instead, a refuge from enemies as well as a desirable breeding place. Raccoons also have a proclivity for sun-bathing in trees during bright, warm days.

Although they forage over a diversity of habitats, raccoons are seldom found far from water, inhabiting moist situations, especially streambanks and shorelines. They swim well and also climb with agility.

Raccoons are omnivores, which means they will eat almost anything they can catch or gather. Because they like to be near water, they eat a lot of crayfish, frogs, fish, and mussels. They also eat birds' eggs, grasshoppers, crickets, other insects, and a variety of plants and berries. Although mainly nocturnal, raccoons are known to forage during the day as well.

The breeding season for the raccoon is throughout February. A male may travel many kilometers in search of a receptive female, and once he finds her,

RACCOON / TOM J. ULRICH

RACCOON / TOM J. ULRICH

YOUNG RACCOON / TOM J. ULRICH

he will move into her den and stay for several days while copulation takes place. He then leaves, in search of new conquests; a female, however, is monogamous for the breeding season.

Raccoons prefer hollow trees and logs for homes, but often use the ground burrows of other animals for raising their young or for sleeping during the coldest part of the winter months. After a gestation period of about 63 days, the young are born in April or May, and family life continues throughout the fall and early winter until the breeding season, when the young go out on their own. The male gives no assistance in raising the young.

Winter is the greatest enemy of raccoons in the northern part of their range. Unlike their southern relatives that remain active and feed all winter, northern raccoons exist on the store of fat built up by autumn gorging, which by late fall may comprise about half the animal's total body weight. The high winter mortality rate is offset by a high rate of reproduction. In the north, raccoons average more than four and as high as seven young per litter, compared to an average of two per litter in the southern United States.

Marten

Martes americana

BJKCKNWY

WEASEL FAMILY

Lithe, alert, agile, insatiably curious, excitable, temperamental, and quarrelsome, the marten is a typical member of the weasel family, and is the most arboreal of the bunch. Also called the "pine marten" and "American sable," the marten once inhabited the mature coniferous forest from one coast to the other, all the way to the northern limit of trees.

The marten is much smaller than a fisher and about the same size as a mink, an adult male weighing about 900 g (2 lb) and reaching a length of 60 cm (24 in). Typical of the weasel family, the female is smaller than its mate, although the bushy tail is about 15 cm (6 in) long in both sexes.

The marten's fur is usually a lustrous chocolate brown with darker legs and tail. The best identifying characteristic is the distinctive orange or yellow splash of irregular shape and varying size on the throat and chest. The foxlike head and face are usually lighter in color, and the edge of the catlike ears are white. Individuals vary, however, from almost black to yellow.

Like other mustelids, the marten has a pair of anal glands, but the odor of the fluid does not approach the mephitic essence of the skunk. Another more practical gland is located just under the skin of the belly. Its fluid is rubbed on logs, tree branches, and rocks to mark the marten's territory and announce its presence.

During the winter the marten's feet are thickly covered with hair, providing both insulation for warmth and snowshoes for easier movement over powdery snow. Although the marten is at home on the ground, it is a svelte aerialist, and high-speed chases through the upper story of the forest in pursuit of flying squirrels and red squirrels are common. They do eat squirrels, although the staples in the marten diet are small rodents—lemmings, mice, voles, and woodrats—with the single unrivaled favorite being the red-backed vole. They also eat birds and their eggs, berries such as blueberries, and insects in season. The marten's natural enemies are the equally agile fisher as well as lynx, wolves, and great horned owls.

An adept but solitary hunter, the marten is savagely intolerant of other animals, mellowing in ferocity only during the mating season from mid-July through August. Trappers and other outdoorspeople often say that "two marten invariably equal one fight."

Marten are territorial and use their scent glands to mark boundaries. Males usually maintain the larger home ranges, which often overlap the territories of several females if food is abundant. Although much smaller, a female's territory may have a higher concentration of prey and other food with which to support herself and her growing young.

During courtship, an interval of temporary gentleness, there is much playing and wrestling. Both males and females are polygamous; females

MARTEN / TOM J. ULRICH

MARTEN / TOM J. ULRICH

MARTEN / TOM J. ULRICH

may breed two or three times a day several times during a breeding season. Some males may be rapacious at this time, causing injury to females as well as rival males.

Despite the diminutive size of the female, her gestation period exceeds that of a moose. This is caused by delayed implantation of the fertilized ovum, a characteristic common to the weasel family. An average of three young are born in March or April, generally in a hollow snag or an expropriated squirrel's den. Weighing about 28 g (1 oz) at birth, the young are reared solely by the female. Blind at birth, the young get the first view of their world at about five weeks of age.

This seldom-seen carnivore is fairly common in montane and lower sub-alpine forests throughout the Canadian Rockies.

Fisher

BJKCKNY

Martes pennanti

WEASEL FAMILY

Of all its common names—"black cat," "pecan," "Pennant's marten," and "wejack"—the name fisher is least suitable, since the fisher does not fish. The name may reflect its habit of robbing traps baited with fish; being confused with the otter, an expert fish catcher; or from early immigrants who noted its similarity to the European polecat, whose other names include "fitche," "fitch-et," or "fichen."

The fisher is larger than a marten, but considerably smaller than a wolverine. An adult male normally weighs 3.5 to 5.5 kg (8 to 12 lb) with a total length of 90 to 120 cm (36 to 48 in), of which about one-third is tail. Females are about 25 percent smaller.

Fishers have slender, muscular bodies, short legs, black feet, bushy tails, low, rounded ears, piercing black eyes, and pointed noses. Like other members of the family, their anal sacs emit a foul-smelling musk.

Their lustrous fur varies between seasons and sexes, and among individuals. Females have a darker brown and silkier fur than males. The coarser coat on males often appears to be "frosted" or grizzled around the head and shoulders, an effect caused by tricolored guard hairs that have a white subterminal band. A small white patch is sometimes discernible on the throat or chest. In

FISHER / TOM J. ULRICH

FISHER / TOM J. ULRICH

both sexes, the fur becomes darker toward the rump and tail. Pelage in the spring and summer is lighter in color and less dense than during the winter.

Possibly the swiftest and most agile member of the weasel family, the fisher is mainly a nocturnal hunter and is active all year. As a hunter, the fisher is largely an opportunist, the diet varying with available prey. The snowshoe hare and porcupine are staples of its diet; other food includes squirrels, mice, shrews, birds, carrion, and fruits. It is the only animal that effectively preys upon porcupines. Repeatedly biting the porcupine's unprotected face, it then flips the animal over to chew through the soft underbelly. Because of its value in controlling porcupines in commercial forests, the fisher has been reintroduced in several areas. Due to its agility, both on the ground and in trees, the fisher has virtually no natural enemies.

One curious thing about the fisher is the way it reproduces. A female, believed to be polygamous in the wild, normally breeds at the age of one year and she remains pregnant throughout most of her life. She mates in the early spring and the embryo remains in a state of suspended growth for several months until normal development resumes. The gestation period of about 352 days is the longest of any mammal in the Canadian Rockies. This seems like an unusually long gestation period for such a small animal, but it is actually due to an intriguing phenomenon, common among mustelids, known as delayed implantation. The blastocyst is not implanted in the uterus until spring, so that the young are not born and raised during the cold winter weather. Parturition is common from March to mid-April, followed almost immediately by breeding again. Fisher normally produce an average of three young per litter, which are helpless, sparsely furred, and weigh about 40 g (1.4 oz) at birth. The young start crawling at about eight weeks of age, when their eyes open.

This seldom-seen mammal is rare in the southern part of the Canadian Rockies and occasional in the north. Its low profile is due primarily to its choice of densely wooded habitat, restricted range, and low population densities. Only the luckiest or most persistent visitor will see the elusive fisher in its subalpine forest habitat.

Ermine

BJKCKNWY

Mustela erminea

WEASEL FAMILY

The ermine, often called the "short-tailed weasel" or "stoat," displays the characteristic long, slim body, small face, long neck, and short ears of the weasel family. Males, averaging 30 to 40 cm (12 to 16 in) in length, are about twice as large as females. The tail is about one-third the length of the body, and this short tail and smaller size help to distinguish the ermine from the long-tailed weasel.

During the summer, ermine sport a two-tone pelage of chocolate brown on top with a whitish to sulfur yellow color below. With the advance of winter, the coat changes to a spotless white except for a terminal black tip on the tail.

Ermine seem to be constantly seeking food, an adult consuming about

ERMINE IN SUMMER PELAGE / TOM J. ULRICH

ERMINE IN WINTER PELAGE / TOM J. ULRICH

one-third of its weight every day. Although small rodents constitute the main diet, these are supplemented by birds and their eggs, squirrels, fish, frogs, and insects. A ferocious hunter, the ermine occasionally takes prey such as hares, many times its own size. With a slender body and a keen sense of smell, it can easily move through small burrows in nocturnal pursuit of rodents. A good climber, it also chases squirrels and chipmunks, and in winter, often forages beneath the blanket of snow.

Home range size varies with the season, food supply, and sex, and may be two to three times larger during periods of rodent scarcity than during rodent abundance. Females occupy smaller territories than males and both defend their home ranges against others of the same sex.

This weasel is usually solitary except when it is mating and when the female is caring for its young. Mating behavior is prolonged in weasels. Vigorous fighting prior to breeding is typical, followed by copulation that may last a few hours and occur repeatedly over the breeding cycle. Although mating occurs in early summer, implantation is delayed. In the spring, after a lengthy gestation, four to nine young are born in a nest lined with grass and fur, often located in a hollow log. Blind and deaf and quite helpless at birth, the kits have string-bean-like bodies with a few white hairs along the neck and back. At about one month of age, their ears and eyes open and their coats are fully grown. Young weasels are playful and spend a great deal of time playfighting. Growth is rapid, with the males becoming larger than their mothers in about seven weeks. The larger males use different food sources and thus reduce competition between the sexes.

Ermine are preyed upon by hawks, owls, and foxes. Humankind, however, is the most serious enemy, trapping them for fur and destroying their habitat.

Ermine are the most common weasel in the Canadian Rockies. They seem to prefer habitats in subalpine meadows and adjacent forests, but since they are primarily nocturnal, ermine are seldom seen.

Least Weasel

Mustela nivalis

BJKCNW

WEASEL FAMILY

The least weasel is the smallest of all living carnivores, fully grown individuals measuring only 15 to 20 cm (6 to 8 in) from nose to tip of tail. Its tail is a mere 2.5 to 3.8 cm (1 to 1.5 in) long and lacks the pronounced black tip common to other weasel species in the Canadian Rockies. Its small size, small ears, and short tail without a black tip readily distinguish it from the ermine and long-tailed weasel.

While the winter pelage is entirely white, the summer pelage is a rich chocolate brown on the upperparts with white on the underparts. The change to summer pelage takes place from late April to early May.

The least weasel is primarily a mouse hunter, but its food includes other small rodents, shrews, insects, amphibians, and small birds. It has an enormous appetite, consuming about half its body weight each day. In turn, it has a number of enemies, including hawks, owls, foxes, coyotes, and long-tailed weasels.

This weasel has well-furred feet for protection at low temperatures, and spends the coldest days in its fur-lined den.

Habitat and breeding behavior of the least weasel are similar to those of the ermine, although their home ranges are smaller, generally less than 2 ha (5 ac). Breeding begins as early as February and continues until November. The gestation period is roughly 36 days, with no delayed implantation, as experi-

LEAST WEASEL WITH PREY / S. MASLOWSKI

enced by the other weasels in the Canadian Rockies. More than one litter, therefore, may be produced in a year. From three to ten babies can be born in each litter, but four or five is more usual. The kits are hairless and their eyes and ears are closed at birth. Within two weeks they are well furred; within four weeks their eyes and ears function; and within six weeks the youngsters are weaned. Females are sexually mature at four months of age and males at eight.

While widespread, the least weasel has a rather spotty distribution. This highly energetic creature is occasional from Jasper National Park northward; it is rare on the eastern slopes to the south.

Long-tailed Weasel

Mustela frenata

BJKCWY

WEASEL FAMILY

The long-tailed weasel is the largest of the three species of North American weasels. Males are about 45 cm (18 in) long, including the 16 cm (6 in) tail, and weigh 100 to 200 g (4 to 8 oz). Females are generally 5 cm (2 in) shorter and about 20 percent lighter, but the difference in size varies from region to region. This species occurs only in the New World, ranging throughout southern

Canada from New Brunswick to British Columbia, south to Bolivia and Peru.

In the summer, long-tailed weasels are a rich cinnamon brown above and sulfur yellow to whitish below. In winter, however, the pelage is a uniform snow white, enabling the animal to blend into its surroundings. The tip of the tail remains black throughout the year. The two molts, one in spring and the

LONG-TAILED WEASEL / TOM J. ULRICH

LONG-TAILED WEASEL CARRYING YOUNG / TOM J. ULRICH

other in autumn, are triggered by the amount of light received through the weasel's eyes, which causes certain glands to stimulate molt. In the autumn, the cells in the hair follicles do not contain pigment; hairs grown from such follicles are consequently white. The autumn molt starts first on the belly, moving up the sides, and finally over the animal's upperparts. In the spring, the reverse process occurs, but the hair-forming cells have pigment. Interestingly, the animal does not change to a white coat during winter in the southern portion of its range.

The weasel's forelegs are notably short, and these stubby legs on a long, serpentine body result in a peculiar gait. The weasel's back is arched so high that its hind feet come down nearly in the tracks left by its forefeet, resulting in a bounding, inch-worm-like gait. Although largely terrestrial, weasels can also climb and swim.

In relation to its size, the long-tailed weasel is perhaps unequaled among mammals in its effectiveness as a predator. It kills a wide variety of small-to-medium-sized prey, some much larger than itself, its long, daggerlike canine teeth efficiently stabbing a victim to death. The weasel often strikes at the base of the victim's skull, where its needle-sharp teeth penetrate the brain.

The weasel has a high food requirement. Relying to a great extent upon scent, this superpredator hunts by day or night, killing, at times, more animals than can be immediately consumed, and storing the surplus for possible future consumption.

Breeding behavior of the long-tailed weasel resembles that of the ermine. Although weasels mate in summer, the implantation of the embryo is delayed until the following spring, with the interval between implantation and parturition being about 27 days. Usually, four to eight young are born per litter. At birth the young are blind, toothless, pink, wrinkled, and almost naked. At about five weeks of age their eyes open, and weaning begins soon afterward. The kits remain with their mother until early autumn.

Predators include the wolf, fox, coyote, bobcat, and lynx, as well as hawks, owls, and humans. The black tail tip of this mammal may help to deter predators. Hawks, for example, may strike at the black tip of the tail rather than at the body, allowing some of the intended victims to escape.

Although the long-tailed weasel is occasional in open country from montane meadows to the alpine zone, it is wary of people and is seldom seen. Considered a threatened species in Canada, this weasel is more common than that designation would suggest.

Mink

BJKCKNWY

Mustela vison

WEASEL FAMILY

Mink are found across mainland Canada south of the treeline. In size and construction, they look like large weasels. Mink are semi-aquatic, using waterways for travel as well as a major source of food and shelter. Their preferred habitat is sandwiched between their two cousins, the aquatic river otter and the terrestrial weasel; mink are able to make the best of both worlds.

Approximately the size of a small house cat, males average about 65 cm (26 in) in length and weigh about 1.3 kg (3 lb). They possess a long, thin neck and a slender, muscular body with short, sturdy legs, their tails making up about a third of their total body length. Females are considerably smaller. The fur is soft and glossy—a rich chestnut brown above and paler underneath—with a few white patches on the chin, throat, chest, and abdomen. Unlike the

MINK / TOM J. ULRICH

weasel, the mink does not change to a white coat during the winter. But like all its cousins, it has well-developed anal scent glands that emit a liquid with a strong, musky odor.

Mainly nocturnal, mink are wary and wily animals. The males are solitary and unsociable except during the breeding season, and both sexes select indi-

MINK WITH TROUT / TOM J. ULRICH

vidual home territories that they scentmark and actively defend against other mink.

Mink are excellent swimmers, able to swim 30 m (100 ft) underwater and dive to a depth of 5 m (16 ft) in pursuit of prey.

The mating season occurs from late February to early April, with whelping between late April and the middle of May, often in an abandoned muskrat den. The litter size averages about four. Kits are altricial at birth, weighing only 8 to 10 g (0.3 oz). Their eyes open in about three weeks, and they grow rapidly and may attain 40 percent of their adult body weight and 60 percent of their body length by seven weeks of age. Kits are playful, constantly attacking and squealing at each other, until they leave in the autumn to establish their own territories.

Hunting as much in water as on land, mink enjoy a varied diet of insects, small rodents, frogs, small birds, waterfowl, fish, and muskrats. They are adaptable predators and often cache surplus food for later use.

MINK / TOM J. ULRICH

The best places to see mink are marshlands or along lakeshores, rivers, and streams. They are fairly common in such areas in the Rockies, but are seldom seen because of their largely nocturnal habits. During the day they are most often seen as fast-moving shadows at the water's edge near dusk or dawn.

Wolverine

Gulo gulo

BJKCKNWY

WEASEL FAMILY

The largest land-dwelling member of the weasel family, the wolverine is an animal with many nicknames—"evil one," "Indian devil," "glutton," "devil bear," "skunk bear," and "carcajou." These sometimes bold and pugnacious creatures have the reputation of being one of the greatest troublemakers in the animal world—robbing traps, destroying cabin interiors and eating whatever is edible. Not all of this unsavory reputation is deserved, however, and its dogged determination to survive deserves our respect.

In both appearance and size, a wolverine closely resembles a bear cub; it even moves in a similar manner, with the head and tail generally being carried lower than the somewhat arched back. An adult male wolverine measures more than 1 m (40 in) in length from the tip of its pointed nose to the end of its bushy tail, stands about 40 cm (16 in) high at the shoulder, and is a 15 kg (33 lb) bundle of combative power. This mammal's upperparts are a rich, dark brown, its sides marked with distinct, pale brown to yellowish lateral stripes, which begin over the shoulders, sweep along the flanks, and narrow over the tail. The underparts are pale brown spotted with creamy white; long, coarse guard hairs cover the dense underfur. Although their coats are shed during the year, the color does not change with the seasons. Extremely strong jaws and massive

WOLVERINE / TOM J. ULRICH

teeth are admirably capable of ripping frozen meat and crushing bones, and bearlike paws equipped with five semiretractable claws are well suited for climbing trees, ripping open logs, or disemboweling prey.

Elusive and furtive, the wolverine is solitary for much of the year. Males may cover a home range of 2000 km² (772 mi²), while females range over 500 to 1000 km² (193 to 386 mi²). During the winter their large feet become covered with hair, which creates perfect snowshoes for their extensive treks.

WOLVERINE / TOM J. ULRICH

Wolverines are omnivorous and primarily scavengers, depending on carrion during much of the year, but particularly in winter. They possess an extremely keen sense of smell that helps them locate food even under deep snow. In the summer they consume a much wider variety of food, including wild berries and roots.

Wolverines meet during the summer to mate, drawn together by markings of their foul-smelling musk. Implantation of the embryos is delayed so that most young are born in February or March, often in an underground den lined with leaves. One to six young may be born, but the average litter size is three. At birth the babies have closed eyes, unerupted teeth, weigh about 84 g (3 oz), and are covered with fine whitish hairs, except for darker furred paws. The young grow rapidly and are weaned at about eight weeks, although they may continue to associate with their mother for several months after that. She takes them on hunting trips and may allow them to den with her until the next litter is born.

Wolverines are occasional in the rugged, relatively inaccessible mountains within the Rockies. They tend to trek to high, cooler areas in the summer, although they may be seen in nearly any habitat. You have a reasonable chance to see this much vilified animal around the Lake Louise area in Banff National Park and the Lake O'Hara area in Yoho National Park.

Badger

Taxidea taxus

BKCKW

WEASEL FAMILY

The badger is a heavy-bodied, powerfully built predator with short forelimbs and widely curved front claws about 3 cm (1 in) long. It has a distinctive, flattened body shape, a short, muscular neck, short ears, and short tail. The head is triangular in shape, broad between the ears and tapering to a pointed snout. It possesses two small glands at the base of the tail that can produce a noticeable odor.

The dorsal pelage is coarse and longer than that on the belly. The hair on the underparts is creamy to buffy white, and although the dorsal hair is a similar color at the base, it has a subterminal black band and white tip, giving it a frosted or grizzled appearance. The short hair on the head is adorned with a unique pattern. The muzzle, crown, and hind neck are black to dark brown divided by a white line running from the muzzle to the shoulders. There are white markings on the cheeks as well as a black crescentic spot behind each of them. The white ears are also trimmed with black. A badger averages about 10 kg (22 lb) in weight and about 75 cm (30 in) in length.

BADGER AT DEN / TOM J. ULRICH

Gram for gram, the badger may be the animal kingdom's most efficient digging machine. It loosens the soil with its broad front feet and in one continuous motion sends the dirt flying backwards with its powerful hind legs and feet. A badger can tunnel out of sight in only a minute or two. It goes underground to hunt for prey, to hide from potential enemies, to rear its young, and to rest.

Badgers inhabit open grasslands, farmlands, and parklands. Their food consists mainly of Columbian ground squirrels, Richardson's ground squirrels, northern pocket gophers, mice, voles, ground-nesting birds, and insects.

The badger's home range size varies considerably with different habitat characteristics, prey densities, and sex of the user. Males maintain the larger areas, and although a female's territory may overlap that of other females, males do not infringe on each other's home ranges.

BADGER / TOM J. ULRICH

Badgers mate in the late summer, although delayed implantation of the embryos extends the gestation until March or April. Two to five kits are generally born; they open their eyes at about five weeks of age and are weaned at about two months. The nursery den is usually considerably larger than other badger burrows.

The long claws, sharp teeth, strong, viselike jaws, and thick, loose hide make them an awesome opponent for most predators, and they have, therefore, few natural enemies.

Though not true hibernators, badgers become fat in the autumn and may retire for several weeks during the cold of winter.

Badgers are only occasional in the Canadian Rockies from the Bow River south on the eastern slope and from about Valemount south on the western slope. They are primarily nocturnal, although daytime excursions are not unusual.

Striped Skunk

Mephitis mephitis

JKCKNWY

WEASEL FAMILY

Well known to most North Americans, either from firsthand experience or by reputation, the striped skunk's scientific name—*mephitis*—can be loosely translated from Latin as "bad" or "noxious odor." The chemical armament of this animal is produced from an oily, yellowish liquid with a high sulfur content. The active organic ingredient of the musk is butylmercaptan, which is perceptible to humans at a concentration of less than one-trillionth of an ounce. The musk is produced in two grape-sized glands located on each side of the rectum. Connected to twin nipples by ducts, those glands contain about a tablespoon of musk, which is fired from the exposed nipples only when the tail is raised. The skunk is not an impulsive creature, and only if all else fails does it bend its supple body into a U-shaped position, both head and tail facing the same direction as it draws a bead on its victim. Accurate within 3 m (10 ft) of the enemy, the skunk has enough musk for five or six dousings, each releasing a fine spray, which may cause severe smarting of the eyes for a few minutes. Although all mustelids have such glands, only the skunk uses them as a defensive weapon.

An adult is about the size of a large domestic cat, weighing around 2.5 kg (6 lb). It has a rather small, black head with a white stripe between the eyes,

STRIPED SKUNK / TOM J. ULRICH

MAMA STRIPED SKUNK WITH FOUR STINKERS / TOM J. ULRICH

and glossy black fur overlaid with twin white dorsal stripes that merge at the shoulders and at the base of the tail, a handsome, 20 cm (8 in) long, black-and-white plume. The body is broad and the legs are short, with long, sharp, non-retractable claws used for digging.

The striped skunk is an adaptable animal, preferring the bush corners of meadows, the edge of forests, and open fields with cover near water as habitat. Its appetite is equally adaptable, with the greater part of its diet consisting of grasshoppers, beetles, worms, and grubs of various kinds, as well as fruit, grain, and birds' eggs.

Though not true hibernators, skunks do take long winter naps, the females and young tending to remain underground in their den for a longer period than the males. They may den alone or in any combination of sexes and ages.

Skunks mate after emerging from their dens in the spring. Their sex life is downright tempestuous. Following a hectic courtship, during which rival males occasionally spray one another and growl and claw at each other, vigorous mating takes place. After several copulations, each lasting from 5 to 20 minutes, the female prepares a home for the expected young. Two months after the breeding season, a litter of five to seven kits, each weighing about 28 g (1 oz) is born, thinly furred, wrinkled, blind, and unscented. Within three weeks, their scent sacs develop, along with a thick coat of fur. Kits are nursed for about six weeks before following mom to the field to learn hunting skills. The offspring usually become independent and disperse by autumn.

The striped skunk is fairly common in the extreme southern part of the Canadian Rockies and scarce farther north. It prefers grassy or shrubby habitats in the montane zone.

River Otter

Lutra canadensis

WEASEL FAMILY

A graceful relative of the weasel, the river otter has a long, tapered, muscular body that is well adapted to an aquatic lifestyle. Its head is broad, comparatively small, and somewhat flat; its eyes and ears are small; its bulbous nose large and conspicuous. It has short, powerful legs and a long, tapered tail. Each fur-soled foot has five toes joined by webbing for greater swimming efficiency. Otters have sensitive whiskers, 5 to 10 cm (2 to 4 in) in length, which help detect food in water. Their fur is short and very dense, often considered by furriers among the finest and most desirable for durability and strength. The animal's back is a rich, dark brown while the belly, throat, cheeks, and chin are light tan. Adults may reach 1.1 m (43 in) in length, including a 40 cm (16 in) tail, and usually weigh from 6 to 10 kg (13 to 22 lb).

Though they are occasionally found in lakes, ponds, and marshy areas, river otters are most at home near rivers and streams, and establish territories of various sizes depending on the abundance and availability of food. While the home ranges of females, yearlings, and nonbreeding adults may overlap extensively, adult males defend their territories from other breeding males.

A major means of communication among river otters is scentmarking with feces and urine, as well as musk from a pair of glands located near the base of the tail. They also make a variety of sounds, including chuckles, grunts, chirps, and a shrill whistle.

Perhaps the most playful creature of the animal world, much of the otter's behavior appears to be play. A favorite pastime is repeatedly sliding down

RIVER OTTER / TOM J. ULRICH

mossy or muddy slopes or snow slides along the banks of streams. Choosing a smooth slope, they spread out their hind legs and toboggan on their bellies into the water.

The otter is an accomplished diver and swimmer, spiralling through the water with lithe movements of the body and tail. It may remain submerged for four minutes at a time and dive to depths of more than 10 m (33 ft). Its speed and agility in water allows otters to outmaneuver and catch fish, primarily "trash" fish such as suckers. Although fish make up the majority of the river otter's diet, it also eats mammals, birds, frogs, crayfish, insects, and vegetation, often floating on its back like a sea otter while eating.

Otters usually mate during the spring, while swimming. After a long delay before implantation of the eggs, two to four pups are born a year later in a den located in a hollow log, brush pile, bank, or an abandoned beaver lodge. Young

river otters are from 10 to 12 cm (4 to 5 in) long at birth, fully furred, and have their eyes closed for about the first month. Pups are weaned after two months, but remain with their mother until the next breeding season before striking out on their own.

River otters are occasional from Jasper northward and rare to the south. Because of their secretive nature, river otters are not often seen, but those fortunate enough to view them in the wild will not soon forget the experience.

Cougar

BJKCCKNWY

Felis concolor

CAT FAMILY

The cougar is a cat with many names, including "catamount," "Indian devil," "mountain lion," "panther," "painter," and "puma." At one time, the cougar had the most extensive distribution of any terrestrial mammal in the Western Hemisphere, ranging from the southern Northwest Territories and Yukon in northern Canada to as far south as Patagonia in South America, and from the jungles of Central America to the everglades of Florida. It is either gone forever or greatly reduced in numbers from many of its former haunts, particularly in eastern North America.

Like other cats, the cougar has a lithe, compact, muscular, and deep-chested body with a small head, rounded ears, large eyes, and well-developed whiskers. When the long, slender body is seen in profile, the hindquarters are noticeably higher than the shoulders. Essentially unpatterned with spots or stripes, the coat color gave rise to the name *concolor*, meaning "all of one color." The coat is fairly short and varies in color from gray brown to tawny, with darker tones along the back; the chest, throat, chin, whiskers, and belly are a lighter buff white. The backs of the ears are black and there are dark marks above each eye. Black (melanistic) or white (albinistic) individuals are rarely reported. Unlike those of the bobcat and lynx, the cougar's ears are not tufted. One of its most distinctive characteristics is its long, black-tipped tail, which is a marked contrast to the very short tails of the other two members of the cat family in the Canadian Rockies. As big around as a man's forearm, the cougar's tail is used for balance. Male cougars vary in length from 170 to 275 cm (67 to 107 in), the tail length from 65 to 90 cm (26 to 35 in), and body weight from 60 to 80 kg (132 to 176 lb) or more. Females are generally considerably smaller and lighter. Of the nine cat species found in the Western Hemisphere, the cougar is second in size only to the jaguar of the southwestern United States and Central and South America.

Adult cougars are solitary animals, each occupying an established home range, the boundaries of which are marked by scratching on trees, discharging urine, or leaving scats at boundary points. These scent posts are called scrapes. Although fighting may occur while establishing home ranges, the scent posts are generally sufficient to keep transient males on the move. Home ranges vary considerably in size, depending on the sex and age of the cougar, season of the year, and abundance of prey. Recent studies on the eastern slopes of the Canadian Rockies indicate that individual adult females occupy annual home ranges of about 160 km² (60 mi²), with considerable overlap on the home ranges of neighboring females. Males, on the other hand, have home ranges of between 400 and 850 km² (154 and 328 mi²), which overlap those of one to several females. In contrast to the females, neighboring males have much less overlap in home ranges. Males are known to cover up to 50 km (30 mi) of their range in a single day.

COUGAR / TOM J. ULRICH

COUGAR / TOM J. ULRICH

Cougars are seldom vocal. They emit a yowl during the breeding season and make birdlike whistles when communicating with each other at other times of the year. They also purr loudly; as with domestic cats, this is perhaps a sign of contentment.

Although the cougar has adapted to many habitats in the past, its stronghold is now wild places in mountainous terrain and in the dense boreal forest where the impact of humans is slight. Their preferred habitat is essentially that of their primary prey—the mule deer.

This cat-of-many-names is a highly specialized carnivore, an extremely efficient killing machine. Formidable killing tools include 5 cm (2 in) long canine teeth and scissorlike carnassials designed for biting and shearing. The strong jaws and a short, stubby muzzle allow for an extensive gape with great crushing power. In addition, it has razor-sharp retractile claws on its front feet.

Because a cougar has little stamina, it cannot engage in long chases in the pursuit of prey and depends, instead, on ambush, stalking skills, and a sudden burst of power. Hunting primarily by sight and hearing, a cougar stalks close to its prey and then attacks in powerful bounds, springing onto the back of its prey, severing the neck vertebrae with its teeth, ripping open the throat and windpipe with its claws, and pulling the prey's head back until the neck snaps. Such attacks cause almost instant death, and are so lethally efficient that the cougar can kill prey four times its own size.

The aforementioned study of cougars in the Canadian Rockies indicated that members of the deer family made up nearly 75 percent of their diet. Deer, primarily mule deer, made up 58 percent, moose represented 24 percent, and wapiti comprised 18 percent of all cervids killed. Other prey included beavers,

COUGAR SHARPENING CLAWS / TOM J. ULRICH

porcupines, bighorn sheep, coyotes, snowshoe hares, and grouse. Although exceedingly rare, cougar attacks on humans are known, and a few fatal attacks, mostly on children, have been recorded in North America. Most cougars involved in attacks on humans are either old or sick.

Secretive to the extreme, these big cats give up their solitary existence briefly during the mating period. Females breed about every two years, but unlike most other mammals in the Rockies, breeding may take place during any season. Abandoned by the male immediately after mating, the female gives birth to two to four kittens about three months later. Kittens have a pattern of blackish brown spots and a dark-ringed tail; the pattern

COUGAR / TOM J. ULRICH

COUGAR CATCHING A TROUT / TOM J. ULRICH

gradually fades and is replaced by a tawny coat within a few months. Weighing about 500 g (1 lb) at birth, the completely dependent young feed on their mother's milk for several months. When the kittens leave the den in which they were born, their mother teaches them to stalk and kill game during hunting forays. The kittens may stay with mom for up to 18 months before establishing their own territories. Young cougars reach adult size by the time they are three to five years old. Adult males are polygamous and play no part in raising the family. They can, in fact, be a great danger as they attempt, at times, to eat the kittens.

Although occasional in the montane and subalpine regions of the Canadian Rockies, the elusive cougar is seldom seen. Many people are amply rewarded just by knowing that such a creature exists, or by seeing its tracks in the snow while skiing through its wilderness habitat.

Maintaining a healthy cougar population in the Canadian Rockies will require large tracts of relatively undisturbed wildlands, as well as sound populations of ungulates to supply their food requirements. This superbly efficient predator is part of a rich wildlife heritage and an essential element in nature's plan.

Canada Lynx

BJKCKNWY

Lynx canadensis

CAT FAMILY

Unlike the bobcat, the lynx is a denizen of wilderness areas and symbolizes both the mystery and untamed character of its habitat. A solitary and stealthy creature of the boreal forest, this short-tailed cat has long legs, great moplike paws, prominent ear tufts, and a large ruff of fur surrounding its face. With a black tip on its tail and black ear tufts, the lynx has a luxurious, light gray, slightly mottled winter coat with long guard hairs. The summer coat is shorter with a brownish cast.

Lynx's paws are adapted for traveling over snow, sometimes spreading wider than 10 cm (4 in) in diameter. This large size, combined with the extra fur that grows between its toes and around the edges of its paws during the winter, gives the lynx's feet the characteristics of snowshoes, with about twice

CANADA LYNX / TOM J. ULRICH

CANADA LYNX / TOM J. ULRICH   CANADA LYNX KITTEN / TOM J. ULRICH

the supporting capacity of those of a bobcat. As with other cats, the needle-sharp, retractable claws are used for seizing prey, fighting, and climbing trees.

Although twice the size and weight [8 to 11 kg (18 to 24 lb)] of a large house cat, lynx share many similar characteristics—inquisitiveness, a variety of vocalizations including yowling and purring, an excellent sense of hearing, sight, and smell, and baring the teeth in defense.

Snowshoe hares constitute more than 75 percent of the lynx's cuisine; one animal may eat as many as 200 hares a year. Its extraordinary degree of dependence on a single species for food is illustrated by great fluctuations in lynx numbers over a ten-year cycle. When hares are plentiful, lynx prosper. A year or two after the hare population crashes, few, if any, young lynx survive their first winter. Although the females continue to breed, three to five years may pass before they successfully rear young. The home range of a lynx, which is generally covered in three to six days, may be 13 to 18 km² (5 to 7 mi²) during peak hare numbers, and five times that size during the crashes. Other prey in the lynx's diet include grouse, voles, mice, and squirrels.

Mating occurs primarily in mid-March to May and one to five kittens are born about nine weeks later, often in a hollow tree or rock outcrop. The kittens are blind at birth, their eyes opening in about two weeks. The young remain with their mother through their first winter and actively participate in hunting.

Although this nocturnal cat is fairly common in the Canadian Rockies, particularly in the northern areas, your chances of seeing this secretive creature are slight. An encounter would be a rare and memorable event.

Bobcat

Lynx rufus

KCKNW

CAT FAMILY

Bobcats, or "wildcats" as they are often called, are shy, furtive animals, nocturnal and so reclusive that even biologists who study them may get only infrequent glimpses of the creatures.

Given a choice, a bobcat in the wild will disappear like a ghost when approached by humans. But cornered or trapped, this irascible member of the cat family becomes a hissing, snarling, spitting bundle of claws and fangs. With razor-sharp, retractable claws and formidably long canine teeth, the bobcat, gram for gram, is one of the ablest fighters around.

A male bobcat weighs from 7 to 18 kg (15 to 40 lb), stands about 55 cm (22 in) at the shoulder, and is approximately 80 cm (32 in) in length. Females are about one-third smaller. The bobcat got its name from its short, 15 cm (6 in) tail, which has irregular bars and is black-tipped above and whitish below. A bobcat's fur can vary in coloration, although those in the Canadian Rockies tend to be reddish brown, streaked, and spotted with black. A large ruff of black and white fur surrounds its face; its legs are yellowish brown with black spots; its chest is white with dark markings; and slight tufts of black hair rise from the tips of its ears. Bobcats, however, look a great deal like their cousin the lynx, and even experienced biologists may have difficulty telling them apart in the field. The body of the lynx is more streamlined and its legs are longer. The lynx also has larger paws, its tail lacks black bars, and its coat is a silver gray.

Armed with keen eyesight and excellent hearing, the secretive bobcat catches much of its food by stalking and then attacking in a rush. An adaptable

BOBCAT / TOM J. ULRICH

BOBCAT / TOM J. ULRICH

BOBCAT KITTEN / TOM J. ULRICH

eater, this feline takes whatever food happens to be most abundant and most vulnerable. Rodents, hares, squirrels, and birds are its main fare, although it may also take the occasional deer. Bobcats, in turn, are preyed upon by cougars, coyotes, wolves, and humans.

The resilient bobcat is equally easygoing about where it lives, thriving in virtually any terrain—from suburb to swamp and desert to mountains.

This secretive cat may have a sizable home range, depending on food abundance, available cover, and season. Territorial overlap is greatest among adult males and least among adult females. A male's territory, often overlapping those of several females, may be too large to readily defend, so only places of special significance—rock piles, caves, ant mounds, trails, and rock outcrops—are marked with feces, urine, and scrapes. Females, especially those with young kittens, appear to mark most intensively.

Bobcats in the Canadian Rockies mate in the early spring, the only time during the year when the sexes associate with each other. Two to four spotted kittens are born in a hollow log or rock den after a gestation of about eight weeks. The adult female and her kittens will travel together until the onset of the next breeding season.

Bobcats are occasional, but seldom seen, residents in the Rockies. They are distributed in the southern foothills on the east slopes and from Peace River south on the western slopes.

Rodents

(Order *Rodentia*)

Squirrels (Family *Sciuridae*)
Pocket Gophers (Family *Geomyidae*)
Beavers (Family *Castoridae*)
New World Mice/Rats (Family *Cricetidae*)
Old World Mice/Rats (Family *Muridae*)
Jumping Mice (Family *Zapodidae*)
New World Porcupines (Family *Erethizontidae*)

Most of the mammals in the world, in terms of both the number of individuals and the number of species, are rodents. Of the approximately 4200 species of mammals in the world today, more than 1700, or nearly 40 percent, belong to the order *Rodentia*. They are cosmopolitan in distribution, except for Antarctica.

The primary anatomical characteristics that unite rodents taxonomically are their sets of two upper and lower incisor teeth. Prominent and separated from the molars by a wide gap, or diastema, these chisellike sets of incisors are ever-growing and coated with a hard enamel layer on the front, while the back portion is soft and uncoated. The gnawing action of the rodent wears away the back of the teeth faster than the front, the chewing motion itself thus forming the sharp, chisellike, cutting surfaces of the incisors. Since these teeth grow continuously, rodents must maintain a gnawing and wear schedule to keep them from growing beyond a safe length. Rarely, the teeth continue to grow in a circular course and fatally puncture the afflicted animal's skull. The front of the incisors is often stained red or orange by iron compounds.

The lower jaw is constructed to permit only the incisors—for gnawing— or molars—for grinding—to work at one time, preventing wear against one another. Most rodents chew with a rotary or side-to-side motion of the lower jaw. By drawing the lips together into the gap between its incisors and molars, a rodent can close off the back of its mouth while chewing, thereby excluding unwanted debris, such as nut and seed hulls, soil, and wood, from its diet.

Although rodents are structurally similar, there is great disparity in the size of the animals and their habitat requirements. In the Canadian Rockies, size can range from a 20 g (0.7 oz) deer mouse to a 45 kg (100 lb) beaver. Some members of the order are aquatic or semi-aquatic, some are arboreal, others are terrestrial, and a few are fossorial (mainly living in underground burrows). Some are colonial and others are solitary, some hibernate and others are active all winter. Regardless of their size or habitat preference, rodents are an essential link in the food chain between vegetation and the carnivores.

Within the Canadian Rockies there are 30 species of rodents in seven families. While several are easily visible, others are difficult for even trained biologists to find.

Least Chipmunk
Tamias minimus

BJKCKNWY

SQUIRREL FAMILY

Three species of chipmunks occur in the Canadian Rockies. A casual observer will have considerable difficulty identifying them, but knowing their distribution and habitat preferences will help differentiate among them.

The least chipmunk, the most wide-ranging of the three, has a gigantic range that includes almost all of the Rockies. It prefers moist forest openings and rocky places from valley bottoms to alpine meadows.

The pelage of the least chipmunk is orangy gray, with five black and four contrasting buff white stripes running from the nose to the tail base. It has three dark lines separated by two white lines on each side of its head. The belly is

LEAST CHIPMUNK / GARY R. JONES

white and the fluffy tail, 10 cm (4 in) long, is dark brown above and yellowish below. Adults weigh approximately 50 g (2 oz) and attain an overall length of about 23 cm (9 in). Adult females of the three species of chipmunks occurring in our area are larger than their male counterparts.

Industrious gatherers, least chipmunks definitely prefer seeds for their cuisine, often filling their expandable cheek pouches with prodigious loads of seeds that are sometimes cached for winter survival. When eating, they use their paws like hands.

Torpor lasts from about mid-October to mid-April, and mating takes place soon after emergence. After a gestation period of 28 to 30 days, a litter averaging five pink-skinned young are born, both blind and deaf. Mom cares for the infants for about two months.

All three species of chipmunks in the Canadian Rockies have many enemies. On land they are vulnerable to every carnivore from the diminutive least weasel to the mighty grizzly bear, while from the air they are exposed to attacks by a variety of hawks and diurnal owls.

Since the least chipmunk is active during the day, this chatterbox is a popular entertainer at campsites throughout much of the Rockies, except on the western slopes from Golden to Peace River. An energetic little creature with a flicking tail and wide repertoire of sounds, the least chipmunk is a pleasure to watch as it scampers about its daily affairs.

Yellow-pine Chipmunk

Tamias amoenus

BJKCKWY

SQUIRREL FAMILY

Like other chipmunks, the yellow-pine chipmunk is often nicknamed "chippy" or "stripey." Another nickname, the "buff-bellied chipmunk," relates to the distinctive color of its underparts and is a useful field mark. The yellow-pine chipmunk has bicolored ears that are black on the back and edged with white on the front. Although it generally has a more richly colored coat than the least and a paler coat than the red-tailed, the differences are slight. Adult yellow-pine and least chipmunks are similar in size, weighing about 50 g (2 oz) and measuring approximately 23 cm (9 in) in length.

The yellow-pine chipmunk's diet is about the same as those of the other two chipmunks in the Rockies—primarily seeds with a few berries, fruits, grasses, fungi, and the occasional egg for variety.

Following six months of hibernation, mating takes place soon after emergence in March or April. A litter of about six pups—hairless, deaf, and blind—

YELLOW-PINE CHIPMUNK / TOM J. ULRICH

120

is born about 28 days later. Within three weeks the babies can move about the den, and by five weeks their eyes open. By late summer, the juveniles are grown, and by September or October they are into hibernation.

Although this solitary little chipmunk is territorial to some extent, aggressive behavior is rare. Lactating females, however, may chase intruders away from their denning areas.

This pert little creature is a specialist of dry, open, and rocky habitats from the montane zone to the edge of the treeline. It is fairly common in the southern and central Rockies, but absent in the north.

Red-tailed Chipmunk   W

Tamias ruficaudus   SQUIRREL FAMILY

The best identifying characteristic for the red-tailed chipmunk is its red or rufous tail, especially notable on the underside. Those of the yellow-pine and least chipmunks are tawny to

RED-TAILED CHIPMUNKS / TOM J. ULRICH

ochre colored below and brown above. Although slightly larger than its cousins in the Canadian Rockies, the red-tailed chipmunk has similar reproductive biology, food habits, and enemies.

Found only in the extreme southern Rockies, the red-tailed chipmunk is fairly common in open subalpine forests, particularly among rock-pocked underbrush. It has the most arboreal nature of the three chipmunks in our area.

Woodchuck   KY

Marmota monax   SQUIRREL FAMILY

The woodchuck, or "groundhog," is a member of a group of large, ground-dwelling squirrels called marmots. A marmot has a robust body, short powerful legs, strong claws curved at the tips, and a tail about one-quarter the length of the body. The pelage of the woodchuck is generally a grizzled dark brown on the upperparts and a reddish brown on the underparts, with a bushy, dark brown to black tail. Coloring can be highly variable, including some albino and melanistic occurrences. The adult woodchuck normally weighs about 3 kg (7 lb) and is about 55 cm (22 in) long. It has prominent white teeth, black eyes, and short ears, and a variety of vocalizations, including shrill whistles, hisses, and growls.

Woodchucks are usually solitary animals, although pairs may share the same underground den during the summer. Mating occurs soon after emer-

121

WOODCHUCK / TOM J. ULRICH

gence from hibernation in March or April. A month later, a litter of two to eight, but usually four, young are born blind and hairless. The young emerge from their burrow about six weeks later and are weaned shortly afterward. Both the young and adults put on fat during the summer and usually enter hibernation in late September.

Diurnal creatures, woodchucks are primarily herbivores, eating a variety of green vegetation, including dandelions, alfalfa, and clover. They also eat snails, large insects, and the young of ground-nesting birds. They, in turn, are preyed upon by large carnivorous animals, hawks, and snakes.

Woodchucks usually site their dens on well-drained ridges or slopes where luxuriant grasses and other short-growing plants provide food. Efficient diggers, they generally use different burrows during the summer and winter. Burrows usually have a main entrance, one or more bolt holes for spying enemies, and separate toilet and nesting chambers. These burrows may be as much as 1.5 m (5 ft) deep and 9 m (30 ft) long.

According to folklore, this animal provides us with a weather forecast every year on the second day of February. Although the Groundhog Day forecast is not scientific, it provides the woodchuck with a lot of harmless publicity.

Woodchucks are not present on the eastern slopes of the Rockies and are rare on southern parts of the western slopes. They are generally found along roadsides and other disturbed sites in the montane zone.

Yellow-bellied Marmot

W

Marmota flaviventris

SQUIRREL FAMILY

The yellow-bellied marmot is similar in size to the woodchuck. The fur on the upperparts of the body is grizzled buff brown, while that on the underside

is yellow. The neck fur is light and seems to separate the body fur from the darker fur on the face.

Unlike woodchucks, yellow-bellied marmots live together as family groups in their rocky habitats. Burrows are located well within mountainous talus slopes or in rock piles under cliffs, the boulder-strewn land serving as a

YELLOW-BELLIED MARMOT / TOM J. ULRICH

fortress, preventing large carnivores from digging the marmots out of their burrows. Rarely venturing far from its den, the marmot dashes inside when alarmed, and emits whistles and chirps after it is safely inside. It feasts on grasses and a variety of forbs in nearby meadows, where meals are just a short trundle away.

Litters of three to six young are born in May, after a month's gestation. The siblings spend much of their time playfighting to establish their position in the hierarchy of marmot society. This marmot is sparsely distributed only in the extreme southern portion of the Canadian Rockies.

Hoary Marmot

BJKCKNWY

Marmota caligata

SQUIRREL FAMILY

The hoary marmot, or "whistler" as it is often nicknamed, is the largest squirrel in the Canadian Rockies, with an adult male weighing about 6 kg (13 lb) and attaining an overall length of up to 80 cm (31 in). The female is considerably smaller. The upper pelage is grizzled gray and brown, while the underparts are gray. The name "hoary" refers to the mantle of white fur covering the marmot's shoulders and back. It has contrasting black and white marks on its face, a black "cap" on its head, black feet, and a bushy brown tail.

Hoary marmots live in colonies consisting of a few polygamous males and many females. These marmots are famous for their piercing *"Eeeeeee"* alarm whistle, which is given when danger is detected. After the ear-splitting warning, the entire foraging colony rushes back into the protection of its rocky habitat to escape the unfriendly attention of coyotes, cougars, bears, and golden eagles. This early warning shriek is usually made by a solitary but vigilant sentinel. Marmots may live in colonies so there are more eyes and ears to detect predators.

This wary rock dweller is strictly diurnal, generally out and about even during inclement summer weather. On sunny days, a marmot often lies stretched out indolently on top of a boulder or at the entrance to its burrow. Staples of its diet include grasses, roots, wildflowers, and berries from lush alpine meadows.

Hoary marmots are sociable animals and there seems to be a minimum of friction in a colony. When meeting they often touch noses, mouths, and whiskers, and nuzzle and sniff each other. After these initial greetings, a playful wrestling match may follow. They grapple and wrestle, box with their forepaws, and bite at the fur on each other's head and throat. Animals of both sexes and all ages seem to enjoy and participate in the playfighting.

Hoary marmots spend about two-thirds of their lives hibernating, emerging from their winter dormancy during May, usually before the snow melts. Males find and breed with females in whirlwind romances, with most breeding occurring within two weeks of their emergence. Following a month's gestation, a litter of two to five young are born deep in a grass-lined den. Despite the communal nature of marmot society, the young are cared for exclusively by their mothers, male marmots providing no parental attention. The babies enter the daylight world in late July, but their growth is slow and they are only about half grown when they begin hibernation with their mother in the fall. They grow slowly because of the hostile environment and short growing season for

HOARY MARMOT / TOM J. ULRICH

HOARY MARMOT / TOM J. ULRICH

HOARY MARMOTS PLAYING / TOM J. ULRICH

forage. Although old males and barren females enter their dens in late August, fertile adult females and the juveniles remain active for a few more weeks. This provides the young with extra time to grow and fatten before their critical first year of hibernation. By the end of the third summer the juveniles are fully grown, sexually mature, and usually establish their own burrows. The mothers are unable to store as much fat as the nonbreeding females and are thus in no condition to breed the following spring. Unlike other rodents, reproduction rates for hoary marmots are low since females are three years old before they have their first litter and may not have another for two or more years.

Hoary marmots occur almost exclusively on boulder-filled meadows in the alpine zone and on talus slopes that penetrate the forest. They are common from Banff northward, but less common to the south.

Richardson's Ground Squirrel   KCW
Spermophilus richardsonii   SQUIRREL FAMILY

Although commonly called a "gopher" or "flickertail," the most abundant member of the squirrel family on the prairie is more correctly called the Richardson's ground squirrel. Adults are about 30 cm (12 in) long, including a tail approximately 8 cm (3 in) in length. Adult males weigh about 360 g (13 oz) in the spring but may add 80 g (3 oz) before hibernation. Females are about the same size, but a little lighter. Their pelage—pale yellow sides, brownish back, and pale gray or buff underparts—blends well with the bleached grasses and light-colored soils of the prairies. Large, almond-shaped, black eyes set high in the skull permit them to see airborn predators with a minimum of movement.

This diurnal ground squirrel is colonial in habit, with many families living adjacent to one another. Colonial living provides the advantage of many sentinels to warn of danger. The signal, a high-pitched, repetitive squeak,

RICHARDSON'S GROUND SQUIRREL / TOM J. ULRICH

accompanied by a flick of the tail, is followed immediately by a retreat to the burrows, a complicated network of tunnels with chambers, storerooms, and several entrances and exits.

Emerging from their long winter's nap by March or April, the squirrels breed almost immediately and bear an average of six to eight young in less than a month. The female and her young are indifferent or openly hostile to everyone else in the colony.

Ground squirrels prefer to forage on a variety of leaves, flowers, roots, and seeds, but they also eat grasshoppers, beetles, other insects, and their road-killed kin. They, in turn, are an important item in the diet of numerous predators. Golden eagles, ferruginous hawks, rough-legged hawks, Swainson's hawks, and red-tailed hawks are dangerous avian predators. Coyotes and red foxes take them on the land, while badgers, ermines, and long-tailed weasels attack them in their dens.

Richardson's ground squirrels are numerous on overgrazed pastures, roadside ditches, hay meadows, and grainfields from the Bow River south on the eastern slopes; there are none on the western slopes. These flickertails are one of the easiest animals to observe, silhouetted on a grassy slope or playing "chicken" with traffic on the roads.

Columbian Ground Squirrel

Spermophilus columbianus

BJKCKNWY

SQUIRREL FAMILY

The Columbian ground squirrel can be distinguished from a Richardson's ground squirrel by the rusty tinge to its head and feet, its bushier brown tail with creamy terminal band, pale ginger underparts, salt-and-pepper back coloration, and pale eye-ring. Adults have an overall length of about 35 cm (14 in) and weigh approximately 500 g (1 lb) in peak condition.

Columbian ground squirrels live in a colony subdivided into territories controlled by a dominant male. Several adult females, yearlings, and juveniles of both sexes may be included within a territory. This contrasts with a Richardson's ground squirrel colony, where each female has her own territory and the social structure includes only the female and her offspring. Population density within the Columbian ground squirrel colony varies from 10 to 20 adults per hectare (2.5 ac).

The type of burrow used by Columbian ground squirrels varies with the season, but most are dug in porous soil on sites with southern exposures. The nesting den, usually located near the center of a territory, consists of a single chamber, a bathroom, and a few entrances. The summer den, located near the main food supply, has a main entrance extending downward for about a meter (39 in), which levels off and leads to a central chamber approximately 75 cm (30 in) across. Radiating from the chamber is a network of small tunnels, each with hidden entrances, or bolt holes, for quick escape should a predator appear during the squirrel's daily feeding sorties. In late summer, the burrow is dug an additional meter deeper and the hibernation chamber is lined with dried grasses. The hibernation burrow is wonderfully engineered to drain water away from the sleeping chamber; this is done by digging a sump tunnel half a meter (19 in) deeper than the sleeping chamber. Dens are then dug on side slopes, thus placing the sleeping chamber above the entrance, to prevent the collection of water in the nest. After entering the hibernation den from late August to early October, the squirrel plugs the entrance with soil and curls up, with nose pressed against belly, for the winter, emerging by early April in the valleys, and as late as mid-June in alpine meadows. Males emerge first, followed in about ten days by the females and yearlings.

Mating occurs within three weeks after emergence. A male fights to secure a territory that overlaps those of several females. Confrontations range from flank-to-flank shoving matches to vicious frontal attacks that inflict deep wounds. After mating, the male anchors a plug in the female's vagina to prevent other males from inserting sperm for at least a few hours. After a gestation period of 24 days, from two to seven, but usually four, blind and hairless infants are born, weighing only 9 g (0.3 oz) each. Although the young are weaned and

COLUMBIAN GROUND SQUIRREL / TOM J. ULRICH

emerge from the natal den at the end of their first month, they require two summers to achieve their full body size.

Although Columbian ground squirrels are omnivores, most of their diet consists of a variety of grasses, roots, tubers, leaves, seeds, flowers, and fruits.

COLUMBIAN GROUND SQUIRREL / TOM J. ULRICH

Bulbs of wild onion, lilies, and spring beauties are also staples. Animal matter in their diet includes grasshoppers, caterpillars, and the occasional small mammal and ground-nesting bird. Their enemies, in turn, include badgers, weasels, coyotes, wolves, skunks, buteo hawks, and golden eagles. Grizzly bears, needing to build a huge fat storehouse in autumn before they too succumb to a winter sleep, expend vast amounts of energy digging these hibernators from their dens.

Since these squirrels may carry fleas that harbor bubonic plague, they should not be handled or allowed to climb on you or your children.

Because of its diurnal habits, the Columbian ground squirrel is one of the most conspicuous mammals in mountain meadows at a wide variety of elevations in the central and southern portions of the Canadian Rockies.

Thirteen-lined Ground Squirrel   KCW

Spermophilus tridecemlineatus   SQUIRREL FAMILY

Easily identified, this ground squirrel has a distinctive coat featuring seven brown stripes with buff spots alternating with six beige stripes. Its nose and cheeks are cinnamon colored and it has a pale eye-ring. It should not be mistaken for a chip-

THIRTEEN-LINED GROUND SQUIRREL / TOM J. ULRICH

munk because of its larger size, small ears, less bushy tail, and the lack of facial stripes. Adults are about 28 cm (11 in) in length and weigh about 180 g (6 oz).

The thirteen-lined ground squirrel is not as colonial as some of its relatives; it lives alone or in small family groups. When alarmed it scampers along well-defined runways and disappears into a long, deep burrow.

The escape holes in the burrow are not marked by telltale earth mounds. In addition to a diet of vegetable material, the "thirteen-liner" eats insects, mice, other small animals, and birds' eggs until it becomes very fat, and by September starts nodding off in its underground chambers. Hibernation continues until the mating season in April, and a litter of seven to ten young is born in May.

This "striper" is occasional in the foothills from about the Bow River south on the eastern slopes.

Golden-mantled Ground Squirrel

BJKCKNWY

Spermophilus lateralis

SQUIRREL FAMILY

Golden-mantled ground squirrels are easily identified by the prominent white stripe, edged in black, that runs from the shoulders to rump on each side of the body. The mantle, covering the head, neck, and shoulders, varies from yellow ochre to russet brown, and there are white crescents above and below the eye. The underparts, feet, and legs are buffy.

Apart from the fact that it prefers to live in rocky places within the subalpine and alpine zones, the size, diet, and general life cycle of the golden-mantled ground squirrel are not much different from those of the thirteen-liner, except that its burrows are much simpler.

It is often unnecessary to look for these active little creatures; they will come to you, hoping to be fed. When coaxed with food they can be tamed to the point of boldness, often climbing onto the shoes or legs of delighted humans. Although it may be tempting to reward this friendly squirrel with a handful of trail mix or a few peanuts, don't do it; our food may be harmful for it.

Golden-mantled ground squirrels are common from the northern part of the Willmore Wilderness area and Mount Robson Provincial Park to the south. They are absent only in the extreme northern portion of the Canadian Rockies.

GOLDEN-MANTLED GROUND SQUIRREL / TOM J. ULRICH

129

Red Squirrel

Tamiasciurus hudsonicus

SQUIRREL FAMILY

A tree-dwelling animal, an adult red squirrel weighs 185 to 330 g (7 to 12 oz) and measures 30 to 34 cm (12 to 13 in) from nose to tip of tail. The sexes look alike, showing seasonal color variation. In summer they are rusty red on the upper body and grayish white on the lower, with a prominent black stripe along each side. The tail is red on top and yellow gray on the underside. In winter the

RED SQUIRREL / TOM J. ULRICH

RED SQUIRREL / TOM J. ULRICH

fur becomes rufous and the black stripes disappear, but the white crescents above and below the eyes are constant throughout the year.

Red squirrels are sexually mature at one year of age. Breeding occurs in April, and the young are born near the end of May following 35 days of gestation. Their first few weeks are spent in a nest made from plant fibers; in the Canadian Rockies the nest is almost always underground, not in trees. The average litter size is four, but may range from one to as many as eight. The young are born furless and remain blind for the first month. Young squirrels are weaned at eight weeks, but may stay in mom's care until the end of summer. Second litters in the Rockies are rare because of the short summer season.

Pine and spruce seeds constitute the bulk of the red squirrel's diet, but it also eats nuts, mushrooms, meat, sap, young birds and bird eggs, and a variety of berries. Industrious in the procurement of food, it caches or stores items sometimes in quantities amounting to more than a bushel. Squirrels will habitually return to favorite feeding spots to eat the seeds from spruce and pine cones that they have piled near the base of trees. This activity results in a heap of discarded stems and scales from the cones, which accumulate in middens that may become huge over the years.

The red squirrel is a chatterbox with a variety of calls that serve to advertise its home range and also to announce the presence of intruders. The territorial call is a rolling *"Chrrrr,"* which sounds like a ratchet. It scolds intruders with a long, explosive *"Tchrrrr,"* accompanied by appropriate twitches of the tail. This loquacious character also makes soft *"whuck whuck"* noises as it investigates its territory. Except during the breeding season, it is a solitary creature with a home range of about 1 to 2.5 ha (2.5 to 6 ac).

Red squirrels do not hibernate, but rather stay close to food supplies all winter, often venturing out to feed for a short time at midday even on the coldest days. Enemies besides humans include hawks, horned owls, coyotes, fishers, and martens, the last two easily running down a red squirrel on the ground or in trees.

The squirrel's major habitat consists of mature forests of spruce, pine, and balsam fir, although it can also live quite happily close to people, in cities, towns, and farmyards. Ubiquitous and not at all shy, these noisy little extroverts are probably the most commonly seen wild mammal in the coniferous forest of the montane and subalpine zones.

Northern Flying Squirrel

Glaucomys sabrinus

BJKCKNWY

SQUIRREL FAMILY

Flying rodents? In point of fact, northern flying squirrels would more properly be called gliding squirrels since they glide or volplane and do not actually fly at all. Among the most distinguishing characteristics are their patagia, or gliding membranes. The patagium is a loose flap of skin, fully furred on both sides, extending from the wrist of the foreleg to the ankle of the hind leg. This flap

NORTHERN FLYING SQUIRREL / TOM J. ULRICH

makes it possible for the squirrel to become airborne, and is the animal's gliding apparatus and parachute.

A typical glide begins high in a tree with the animal bobbing its head up and down and from side to side, presumably to aid in distance perception. It launches itself with all four legs spread widely, stretching the patagia to create a flat surface. The tail enlarges the total gliding surface by up to 30 percent and acts as a rudder and stabilizer, but is most important for braking, being thrown upward just before landing to reduce speed and soften the impact. The squirrel can control its direction by raising or lowering a leg or by manipulating its tail. Like a hang glider, its path is downward, traveling forward horizontally up to 1 m (39 in) for every 30 cm (12 in) lost in altitude. Depending on the takeoff height, glides of 45 m (148 ft) are not uncommon. Muscles pull the "wings" over the back once the squirrel has landed, so they do not interfere with normal running and climbing activities.

The northern flying squirrel looks like a red squirrel in a floppy gray overcoat. Its underparts are gray and its back and hindquarters are grayish with a wash of cinnamon brown. Its tail is flat, with the hairs lying outward like vanes on a feather; it is smoke gray above, paler below, and darker toward the tip. Large bulging eyes improve the animal's night vision, and the long sensitive whiskers help it navigate in the dark. The overall length for adults is about 31 cm (12 in) and their weight is approximately 160 g (6 oz).

These furred "frisbees" breed only once a year in the Canadian Rockies—early in the spring—and an average litter of three pups is born during May. At four months the young are proficient gliders and are able to care for themselves.

Strictly nocturnal, flying squirrels are a gregarious lot, particularly during the winter, when groups of a dozen or more snuggle together in a nest to keep warm. They do not hibernate, but are inactive during bitterly cold spells.

This incomparable glider of the night uses two types of dwellings during a year. The interior dens, used during the winter, are woodpecker holes or natural cavities in trees. The summer home, or drey, is outside in the fork of a tree. Covered with fibrous balls of lichen and moss, the drey may be a refurbished magpie nest.

The most carnivorous of the squirrels, the northern flying squirrel's diet includes insects, birds' eggs, nestlings, and carrion, supplemented with seeds of various kinds, fruits, berries, fungi, lichens, and the buds of aspen, alder, and

NORTHERN FLYING SQUIRREL / TOM J. ULRICH

willows. Its main enemies are bobcats, ermine, fisher, lynx, and several species of owls.

The northern flying squirrel is most content among widely spaced coniferous trees in the montane zone. A mysterious creature of the night, this rather common mammal is seldom seen. The best way to see one is to locate a nest during the day and return at night to watch this nimble acrobat sail across the moonlit sky.

Northern Pocket Gopher KCW

Thomomys talpoides POCKET GOPHER FAMILY

Not to be confused with the ground squirrels commonly called "gophers," the pocket gopher spends practically its entire life in a self-constructed burrow system, rarely venturing above ground. It appears on the surface only when dispersing to a new home, searching for a mate, or pushing soil out of the tunnels. Generally, the only sign of its presence is a series of telltale piles of soil dis-

NORTHERN POCKET GOPHER / ALAN G. NELSON

NORTHERN POCKET GOPHER CASTINGS / TOM J. ULRICH

placed from its burrow system. Unlike the burrows of most other mammals, which are left open, the mounds of the pocket gopher are tightly plugged from below to keep out weasels and other predators. This subterranean mammal is continually renovating its tunnel system, digging food storage areas and sleeping chambers, blocking off sections that are filled with fecal material, and excavating feeding tunnels just below the soil surface as it mines for bulbs and roots. During the winter the tunnels are excavated in the snow and packed with soil brought from underground. These ropelike, earthen casts remain after the snow melts, evidence of their wintertime handiwork. The digging activities of these fossorial rodents may play an important role in improving the composition of soils.

The northern pocket gopher is a medium-sized rodent about 22 cm (9 in) long and weighs around 145 g (5 oz). It has fur-lined cheek pouches for carrying food, but unlike chipmunks, these "shopping bags" or pockets are external, extending from beside the mouth down along the sides of the neck. The animal's large, exposed incisors are used as picks in burrowing, but dirt and debris do not get into its mouth because its lips close behind its front teeth. Its body is thickset and strong, covered with very loose skin with soft, brownish hair on the back, and gray hair on the flanks and belly. Built for a life of burrowing in the soil, the northern pocket gopher looks strikingly out of proportion because of its enlarged head, shoulders, front legs, and claws. Its ears and eyes, on the other hand, are disproportionately small.

This pocket gopher forages on roots, tubers, and stems that it cuts and pulls down into the burrow. It eats some food immediately and stores other bits in its pouches, which are emptied by squeezing with the forepaws.

Solitary animals, the males and females associate only during the breeding season, and block off their tunnels to each other after mating. About four young are born, usually in late June or early July, after a 19-day gestation period.

Few people will see this common, subterranean mammal, but its excavating mounds are conspicuous in moist meadows with deep soil. It occurs only in the southern portion of our region.

Beaver

Castor canadensis

BJKCCKNWY

BEAVER FAMILY

The beaver ranges throughout most of North America from the Mexican border to the treeline in Alaska, the Northwest Territories, and Yukon. In Canada, the beaver is found from coast to coast, with the exception of the tundra and some drier areas of the interior. A national emblem of Canada, the beaver's fortune has swung back and forth like a pendulum. At the time of European contact, this mammal strongly influenced the country's development, serving

BEAVER ON LAND / TOM J. ULRICH

as a significant economic entity and the basis of the fur trade that spurred exploration and settlement. After decades of relentless overtrapping and defor- estation, the beaver was nearly extirpated in many areas. With reduced demand for their pelts and some protection, however, beaver numbers have rebounded with a vengeance, and they are now considered a pest in many rural and suburban areas.

The beaver is the heavyweight of North American rodents. The average weight for adults is 16 to 30 kg (35 to 66 lb), but animals over 45 kg (100 lb) have been recorded. Adults are from 100 to 126 cm (40 to 50 in) long, includ- ing a 20 to 50 cm (8 to 20 in) tail. Beavers have large, sharp, front teeth, small ears, and small, beady eyes.

The beaver's most unique feature is its muscular tail—wide and flattened, perhaps 18 cm (7 in) wide and 3 cm (1 in) thick, and covered with leathery scales and sparse hair. Flexible and strong, the tail is used as a rudder while swimming, as a sturdy support on land, and as a counterbalance when the beaver carries heavy tree branches or building materials with its front paws. The beaver makes the most unusual use of its paddlelike tail when it feels threatened, slapping the tail against the water as it dives, making a noise like a pistol shot, to send a warning signal to fellow beavers.

The hind and front feet are different in both structure and function. Broad hind feet with five long webbed toes propel the beaver through the water and support it on soft muddy ground. Each hind foot has split and ser- rated claws that are movable and come together like pliers, serving as a comb for grooming. The beaver's front feet, which are not webbed, are small and dexterous, with long sharp claws suitable for digging and carrying a variety of materials such as sticks, stones, and mud for construction of dams. Secretions

BEAVERS SLEEPING INSIDE LODGE / TOM J. ULRICH

BEAVER LODGE / TOM J. ULRICH

from anal glands, applied to the fur with the hind and front feet, provide water-proofing.

In other ways, too, the beaver is well adapted for aquatic life. Both the nostrils and ears have valves that can be tightly closed for underwater swimming, while the eyes are protected by clear membranes. Oversized lungs enable the beaver to stay beneath the surface for up to 15 minutes. In addition, the lips can be closed behind the long, sharp incisors, permitting the beaver to gnaw underwater. It is a graceful and strong swimmer, either on the surface or beneath it.

Beaver fur is dense, with a thick mat of fine underfur and an outer coat of coarse guard hairs about 6 cm (2.4 in) long. The pelage is generally a reddish brown, but the color may range from pale yellow to black.

Like wolves, beavers may pair for life. The social structure of a beaver colony is based on families consisting of an adult pair and litters from two successive years. The average litter size is four kits, but may range from one to eight. The kits stay with the parents for about two years and are then ousted from the lodge to find mates and establish their own territories.

They eat the buds, leaves, twigs, and nutritious cambium layer of most species of woody plants that grow near water, preferring aspen, poplar, alder, and willow. Aspen bark is a particular favorite—the filet mignon of the beaver world. They also eat herbaceous pond vegetation such as sedges, grasses, and water lilies. While beaver prefer smaller varieties, their sharp, heavy incisors are capable of chiseling away almost any size of tree; anything up to 25 cm (10 in) in diameter can be cut by nature's lumberjack in a matter of minutes. A single beaver may cut more than 200 trees in a year; a family of five or six may require .4 ha (1 ac) of poplar trees for its yearly food supply. During the fall, beavers cache a supply of branches in the water near the lodge or bank burrow to sustain them over the winter.

Nature's engineers, beavers profoundly affect their immediate environment by changing it to suit their needs, with the greatest impact resulting from the construction of dams. The reason beavers build dams is to create a pond deep enough to prevent the water from freezing all the way to the bottom. Dam building usually takes place in August, but repairs are made whenever necessary. Construction begins with the beaver placing sticks in a stream bed, butt-end down into the bottom mud. The first row of sticks is then reinforced with twigs, mud, and stones placed around, between, and in front of the row.

The beaver lodge or house, built in autumn in a natural pond or in a pond formed behind a dam, is another major construction project. Although the structure resembles a pile of sticks, stones, and mud haphazardly heaped together, it is a remarkably functional shelter, large enough to contain one or more chambers, and high enough above the water level to provide dry quarters for the family. There are two or more underwater entrances, placed so that they will be below the ice level in winter. Some beaver houses are merely burrows in a streambank.

Additional engineering activities around the ponds include the construction of canals and runways, used by the beaver to transport food and building material to the pond. Beavers can sometimes be serious pests, flooding fields and roads, and cutting down valuable trees.

Like all rodents, beaver must contend with several predators. Coyotes, wolves, bears, lynx, and wolverines occasionally kill beaver on land, while river otters can swim into the lodge and attack the family group. Mink, hawks, and owls will also take some kits.

The beaver is fairly common throughout the Canadian Rockies, usually colonizing slow-flowing streams, lakes, marshes, and rivers, primarily in forested areas of the montane zone. Although most active between sunset and sunrise, they can sometimes be observed during the late afternoon or on dull or quiet days. Signs that beaver reside nearby include tree stumps with teethmarks, fresh wood chips, dams, lodges, and well-worn paths leading through the underbrush to a river, lake, or stream.

Deer Mouse

Peromyscus maniculatus

BJKCKNWY

NEW WORLD MICE/RATS FAMILY

The deer mouse is quite handsome, as mice go. The best identifying characteristics are its white feet, long, bicolored tail, large eyes, and rather large ears sparsely covered with short fine hairs. Adults have grayish brown fur on the back and sides and a white belly; youngsters have blue-gray upperparts. The general dimensions are 9 cm (3.5 in) for head and body, and 7.5 cm (3 in) for the tail. They weigh about 25 g (1 oz).

These mice usually nest in a stump or underground burrow, where they raise two or three litters a year, with one to eight young in each. Since females

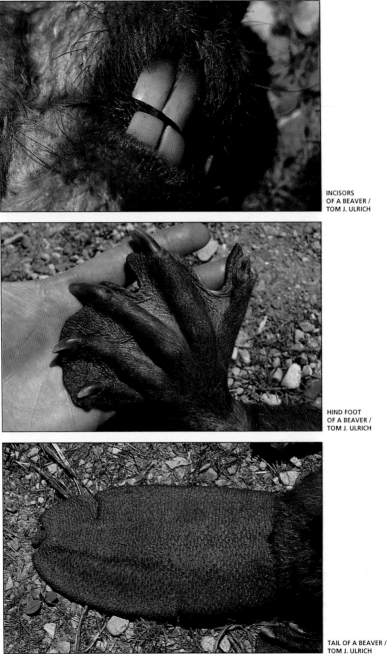

INCISORS
OF A BEAVER /
TOM J. ULRICH

HIND FOOT
OF A BEAVER /
TOM J. ULRICH

TAIL OF A BEAVER /
TOM J. ULRICH

DEER MOUSE / JAN L. WASSINK

are polyestrous, they are pregnant almost constantly during the warmer part of the year, and are quite prolific. Young females are ready to breed at five weeks, males at six. Deer mice often become very abundant and attract night hunters such as owls, weasels, foxes, coyotes, and many other predators, which check their potentially rampant productivity.

Deer mice are active only at night, and their activities can easily be observed with a flashlight. In addition, you can often see their tiny tracks in sand or fresh snow. Much of their activity centers on gathering food. Although partial to seeds, they take whatever is in season locally, including plant greens, fruit, mushrooms, lichens, and insects. In the winter, deer mice may sleep together in a heap to conserve warmth.

Admirably adaptable, deer mice are everywhere throughout our region from the dry valleys to alpine meadows.

Bushy-tailed Woodrat
Neotoma cinerea

BJKCKNWY

NEW WORLD MICE/RATS FAMILY

The bushy-tailed woodrat resembles an overgrown deer mouse, except for its long, bushy tail. Variable in color, most are pale gray-brown to blackish above and whitish below. Juveniles are more blue-gray on the back. About 40 cm (16 in) long, including the tail, which can be as much as half the total body length, they weigh around 350 g (12 oz).

Common, but seldom seen in our area, the bushy-tailed woodrat inhabits cliffs, rock crevices, talus, caves, and abandoned mines and cabins. Yellowish white stains on the rocks are signs of habitation by generations of these animals that have urinated there. A ramshackle nest built with sticks, bark, stones, and a wide variety of other things will be nearby. Over the years, the home grows larger and larger to accommodate its ever increasing pile of acquisitions. Beneath the rubble the nocturnal rodent builds its sleeping chamber, nursing chamber, storage area for food, and a "bathroom."

One of nature's true collectors, the woodrat's big passion for moving things around has given rise to the nickname "packrat." Since it sometimes leaves an object in exchange for the one taken, the creature has earned another nickname—"traderat." But the "trade" is really only a substitution of one item for a more interesting object, and arises because of the animal's mania for carrying things in its mouth. And contrary to many folktales, woodrats are not uniquely motivated to pick up shiny articles.

Each woodrat has its own private den, usually in a rock crevice or cave, or under boulders or a building. Good dens may be occupied by 20 to 30 successive generations, and some dens become huge over the years. Females tolerate other members of their sex in the neighborhood, but males are more solitary, each trying to exclude other males from as large an area as possible by marking its domain with anal musk glands and fighting viciously. They are, however, gentle with their ladies, nuzzling and purring to them before mating.

BUSHY-TAILED WOODRAT / TOM J. ULRICH

Predators include hawks, owls, and a host of carnivorous mammals.

These woodrats are mainly herbivorous and remain active throughout the year. They are extremely agile in running, climbing, and jumping. Although seldom communicating by voice, they thump their hind feet on the ground, particularly when alarmed. Infant woodrats, normally about four to a litter, have specially developed teeth that allow them to grasp the mother's nipples, and therefore get dragged along whenever mom decides to move.

Southern Red-backed Vole   BJKCKNWY

Clethrionomys gapperi   NEW WORLD MICE/RATS FAMILY

The two species of red-backed voles in the Canadian Rockies are tiny creatures with short legs and tail, fairly large ears, small eyes, and a somewhat pointed nose. They are readily distinguishable from the other voles by a broad reddish brown stripe that runs from the forehead to the base of the tufted tail. The rest of the upperparts are generally brownish in color, but it can vary from sooty gray to bright chestnut. In addition, it has buffy gray sides and a light belly. The color varies according to the season and age of the animal.

The southern red-backed vole has a strong penchant for cool, moist habitats in dense coniferous forests with bogs and swamps, up to mossy talus above treeline. It is active day and night through all seasons, tunneling through the snow during winter. Its varied diet includes fruit, seeds, buds, bark, fungi, stems from shrubs and trees, as well as carrion.

Except for the females and their litters, voles seem rather solitary. Females may be more aggressively territorial than males, who will tolerate overlapping ranges with other males.

SOUTHERN RED-BACKED VOLE / DEAN E. PEARSON

Often nesting under deadfall or among the roots of large trees, the females produce from two to four litters a year, with four to seven young in each. Although they reproduce prolifically, the populations of this vole fluctuate enormously from periodic plagues to scarcity. When abundant, they are an important food source for many predatory birds and mammals. The southern red-backed vole is widely distributed in our area south of the Peace River.

Northern Red-backed Vole   N
Clethrionomys rutilus   NEW WORLD MICE/RATS FAMILY

The northern red-backed vole is extremely similar to its southern cousin. The stripe down the back, however, is a brighter red. They are widely distributed north of the Peace River.

Heather Vole   BJKCKNWY
Phenacomys intermedius   NEW WORLD MICE/RATS FAMILY

This mammal is a grizzled brown on the upperparts, with silvery gray under-parts, and white feet. The bicolored, wirelike tail is short, slender, and thinly haired.

As its name implies, the heather vole is a resident of the heather and blue-berry patches of the alpine zone, but it may also inhabit dry forested areas in the subalpine and montane zones. These voles are mainly nocturnal, but are occasionally seen scuttling about during the day. They nest below ground in winter and above ground in summer. Females have two or more litters of about five young each per season, which they care for without help from the males. Staple foods include the foliage of herbs and shrubs, and they also cache twig buds and bark for winter use.

During summer months, heather voles lead solitary lives, except during the breeding season. Family groups may huddle together in communal nests during the winter. Hawks and owls seem to be the most important predators on this vole, but weasels, marten, and other carnivores pursue it as well.

Heather voles are fairly common south of Peace River and occasional northward.

Meadow Vole   BJKCKNWY
Microtus pennsylvanicus   NEW WORLD MICE/RATS FAMILY

The meadow vole is common in grasslands, marshes, bogs, and cultivated fields throughout the Canadian Rockies. Since it favors moist habitats overgrown with tall grasses and sedges, its home range is often wet or even flooded. This vole builds well-groomed runways through the overhead cover, with different passageways to foraging areas, food caches, and toilet sites. It is an excellent swimmer, buoyed by the air bubbles trapped in its water-repellent fur. It may be active day and night, in any season.

The meadow vole has a long, dense, grayish top coat in winter, which is replaced by a short, less dense, grizzled brown summer coat. The undercoat is dusky gray. The meadow vole weighs about 32 g (1.1 oz) and is 14.5 cm (5.7 in) long, including a 3.8 cm (1.5 in) tail. Its diet consists of a variety of green plants and roots.

Meadow voles live in colonies, with up to 1000 voles per hectare (400 per ac) at peaks in the population cycle. They are pugnacious and maintain tiny inviolate territories around their nests. This vole has one of the highest reproductive rates of any mammal in the Rockies, producing three or four litters of

two to nine young each year. The meadow vole is a major food source for many predatory birds and mammals.

Long-tailed Vole
Microtus longicaudus

BJKCKNWY
NEW WORLD MICE/RATS FAMILY

Except for its slightly larger size and considerably longer tail, as implied by its name, the long-tailed vole closely resembles the meadow vole. The relatively thick tapering tail is about 5.8 cm (2.3 in) long, 35 percent of the total body length, which is very long for a vole. Their life cycles are similar as well. Habitat for the long-tailed vole ranges from marshes and grasslands in the valley bottoms to alpine streambanks and boulder-strewn slopes. It is relatively common throughout our area.

Water Vole
Microtus richardsoni

BJKCWY
NEW WORLD MICE/RATS FAMILY

The largest of the North American voles, the water vole weighs about 160 g (6 oz) and is 25 cm (10 in) in total body length. Reddish brown on the back and gray on the belly, this vole lives in underground burrows in alpine meadows, close to swift, clear streams and other wet places. It is an excellent swimmer, sometimes diving into water to escape from terrestrial predators. Its diet includes asters, lilies, and a variety of other plants in its alpine habitat.

Few details are known about the water vole's life cycle. A female usually bears two litters per season, with an average of five young in each. Females from the spring litter mature in five weeks and bear their own young by mid-summer. At the peak of the population cycle, water voles are beset with waves of hungry predators.

Although it occurs in fair numbers in certain areas, it is generally uncommon in the Rockies.

Muskrat
Ondatra zibethicus

BJKCKNWY

NEW WORLD MICE/RATS FAMILY

Although it shares some characteristics and habitat with beavers, the muskrat is not closely related to them. And in spite of its name and long scaly tail, it is not a rat, but rather a large meadow vole that has adapted to a semi-aquatic lifestyle. The muskrat's name is derived from the musky odor emitted from two anal glands that enlarge during the breeding season. This musky-smelling substance is released in small amounts at numerous points along its travel routes, serving as a means of communication, especially during the mating season.

The muskrat is indigenous and widely distributed throughout most of North America, ranging from the Arctic Ocean to the Gulf of Mexico and from the Atlantic to the Pacific Ocean. Muskrats thrive and are common in almost any wetland situation where aquatic vegetation is available and sufficient water depths exist to prevent complete freezing from surface to bottom during the winter. In rivers and streams, muskrats prefer slow-flowing water associated with oxbows, backwaters, or pools.

MUSKRAT / TOM J. ULRICH

Near the turn of this century, muskrats were introduced to Europe, where they readily established themselves. They are now common in Europe and have spread into northern Asia.

Muskrats have a chunky, paunchy appearance, and except for the scaly tail and feet, the entire body is covered with layers of fur. The short, dense, silky underfur is covered with long, coarse, glossy guard hairs. The muskrat's head and back are dark brown and its belly is a light grayish brown. A full-grown animal weighs about 1 kg (2.2 lb) and is around 55 cm (22 in) long from nose to tail tip.

A casual observer will sometimes mistake a muskrat for a beaver, although the adult muskrat is much smaller than a beaver and its tail is quite different. The beaver has a wide, flat tail while the muskrat's tail, up to 25 cm (10 in) long, is round, slender, and tapered. The muskrat also whips its tail back and forth like a rudder while swimming.

The muskrat is remarkably well adapted to a semi-aquatic life. Adults can swim effortlessly for long periods of time, an ability that is facilitated by the buoyancy of the thick, water-repellent fur and the capacity of the underfur to trap air next to the skin, creating a barrier against heat loss. When cruising on the water's surface, the muskrat uses its tail as a balancing agent, or may stiffen the tail and use it as a rudder. Underwater, the muskrat whips its tail from side to side in a sculling action—forming V-shaped waves in the water—producing both propulsion and steerage, while alternately stroking with its partially webbed hind feet. Besides webbing, there are fringes of stiff hairs on the sides of the toes and hind feet, creating a paddlelike effect.

In addition to being a graceful and accomplished swimmer, the muskrat is also capable of deep dives. During a dive, muscles in the ears, nose, and throat automatically constrict and block out the entrance of water. While an average dive lasts for about 3 minutes, muskrats can stay underwater for more than 15 minutes. Special physiological adaptations help to achieve this endurance. The muskrat has a low sensitivity to high levels of carbon dioxide in the blood. It also has the capacity to store oxygen in the muscles prior to a dive, and can reduce the amount of oxygen it uses by depressing its heart rate and relaxing its muscles when submerged. In addition, its well-developed, heat-generating fat tissue cradles vital organs that would otherwise be vulnerable to the stresses of cooling in frigid water. Extended dives are important in escaping enemies, digging burrows and channels, cutting submerged forage, and traveling long distances under ice. Lips that close behind its incisors are also useful, enabling the muskrat, while submerged, to cut stems and roots of aquatic plants without ingesting water.

Muskrats construct several types of shelters to help cope with a severe environment. The decision to build a lodge or excavate a bank burrow is governed by the resources of the habitat. Where banks of a water body are gently sloping and aquatic vegetation is abundant, muskrats construct lodges each autumn by cutting emergent vegetation and piling it on an existing base such as a log, branch, or cattail clump. Burrowing upward from the bottom to a point

above water level in the center of the pile, the animals then construct a series of chambers, tunnels, and plunge holes. The lodges can be as much as 1.5 m (5 ft) high and 2 m (7 ft) in diameter. During the winter, several muskrats may occupy a lodge, their combined body heat keeping the chamber warmer than the outside temperature, and allowing the plunge hole, or underwater entrance, to remain free from ice.

Where banks are steep, such as along many rivers and portions of ponds or lakes, muskrats excavate burrows into the bank, with two or three entrances leading to one or more chambers.

Another structure essential to the muskrat's winter welfare is a "push-up." Usually made of submergent vegetation from the marsh bottom piled on top of a crack or hole the muskrat chips in the ice, push-ups are miniature lodges with enough room for only one animal at a time. They are spaced at intervals of about 10 m (33 ft), radiating for up to 100 m (328 ft), from either the bank burrow or main lodge. Push-ups increase the muskrat's foraging range beneath the ice by providing stops where it can rest, warm up, renew its oxygen supply, and feed. Channels between the push-ups and the main lodge or burrow are maintained by chewing away the ice. Unfortunately for the muskrat, large ungulates may paw at the push-ups and eat the vegetation.

A muskrat also builds summer feeding platforms from mud and plant leaves so that it can feed out of the water and sun itself. After eating, the muskrat grooms its fur and cleans the platform.

Like most rodents, muskrats can be exceptionally productive, usually becoming sexually active the spring following birth, rarely in the same season they are born. In the Canadian Rockies, breeding begins in March or April, and

MUSKRAT FEEDING PLATFORM / TOM J. ULRICH

during this time the males become extremely aggressive, occasionally fighting rivals to the death. A single female may produce as many as four litters of eight young during a summer, but two litters per female is more common. After a gestation period of approximately four weeks, young are born blind and hairless in burrows, lodges, or on open rafts of vegetation. Young muskrats are forced to fend for themselves at approximately four weeks of age and strike out on their own within six weeks. Males and females are promiscuous or loosely monogamous, with males offering little, if any, parental care.

Muskrats are primarily plant eaters, with foods being chosen on the basis of density, availability, and palatability of particular plant species. They will sample most plants growing at the water's edge, but the roots, leaves, and stems of plants such as cattails, bulrushes, arrowhead, horsetails, and reeds compose the bulk of their diet. Underwater roots and tubers, as well as pondweeds, are important food sources during the winter, when ice prevents muskrats from foraging on land. They may also eat clams, crayfish, frogs, fish, and carrion when these food items are abundant and the supply of high-quality plants runs low.

With the exception of females and their young, muskrats tend to be fairly solitary during the summer months. As winter approaches, their behavior changes and several muskrats may den together in the cold.

Unlike beavers, muskrats do not store food for the winter and consequently must subsist on plants and animals they can find under the ice. The ice depth in winter and water level during the remainder of the year are critical factors controlling muskrat survival and reproduction. Individuals forced to leave their homes by ice or drought conditions become easy prey.

148

Since the fecundity of muskrats is so high, nature has provided a means of keeping them in check. Hawks and owls attack them from the air; coyotes, wolves, and foxes on the land; and pike and mink in their aquatic environment. Mink, in particular, occupying much the same habitat as muskrats, cause heavy mortality among juveniles. Humankind seeking its rich fur, however, is the major enemy. It is not uncommon for 50 to 60 percent of the muskrat population to be lost by January.

Although generally nocturnal, muskrats are also about during the day, especially in the spring and early summer. One of the most readily observed of all Rocky Mountain mammals, the muskrat is common in ponds, lakes with marshy shores, and some slow-flowing streams.

Brown Lemming   N

Lemmus sibiricus   NEW WORLD MICE/RATS FAMILY

The brown lemming is a tundra species that occurs in the alpine, subalpine bogs, and talus in the northern portion of the Canadian Rockies. Weighing about 100 g (4 oz) and measuring 15 cm (6 in) in length, it has a large head, short, furry feet with stiff bristles on the soles and toes, claws specialized for digging, and a stubby tail. The pelage is reddish brown above and gray below.

Brown lemmings live in large colonies, building extensive passageways just under the surface of the soil during the summer, and establishing burrows with several chambers that serve different functions. During the winter they construct runs beneath the snow and build round nests of grass above ground that are exposed when the snow melts. These lemmings forage primarily on grasses and sedges, but in winter they nibble on shrubs that lie under the snow.

BROWN LEMMING / EDGAR T. JONES

Breeding can occur throughout the year, with the exception of an interval during May or June, when they move to higher ground to avoid being flooded by spring melt. They have from one to three litters a year, usually with four to eight young per litter. The lemming population follows a three-to-four-year cycle, with peak populations often being followed by an equally dramatic crash in numbers. When abundant, they are an important item in the diet of several carnivores and raptorial birds.

Northern Bog Lemming

Synaptomys borealis

NEW WORLD MICE/RATS FAMILY

The northern bog lemming is smaller than the brown lemming, weighing about 30 g (1 oz) and measuring about 13 cm (5 in) in length. It has a very short tail, only 2 cm (1 in) long. Its longish fur is grayish brown to brown above and dull

gray below, and its ears are often concealed in the long, rust-colored hair at their base.

The major components of the northern bog lemming's diet are grasses, sedges, and leafy plants. In summer it nests in an underground burrow where the female bears four litters of four or five young each. Like its cousin, this lemming builds spherical nests of dry

NORTHERN BOG LEMMING / DEAN E. PEARSON

grass above ground in winter to take advantage of the insulating value of snow. Summer and winter, it often leaves piles of cuttings as well as feces along its well-marked runways.

One of the lesser-known rodents in Canada, the northern bog lemming does not seem to have the extreme boom-and-bust cycles of its relatives. Several species of carnivores, as well as hawks and owls, prey on this tiny creature.

This lemming is occasional in boggy alpine and subalpine meadows and muskegs in the Canadian Rockies. Usually a scarce animal, it is sometimes common in small localized pockets.

Norway Rat

Rattus norvegicus

OLD WORLD MICE/RATS FAMILY

An immigrant from Asia, the Norway rat is 30 to 45 cm (12 to 18 in) in length and weighs 200 to 500 g (7 to 18 oz). The long, snaked tail is scaly and comprises somewhat less than half the total body length. Its pelage is grizzled brown above and yellowish gray on the underparts.

A commensal species, the sphere of activity for the Norway rat is primarily human habitation in cities, towns, rural areas, and associated facilities such as

NORWAY RAT / JAN L. WASSINK

garbage dumps and sewage systems. The totally omnivorous Norway rat is colonial, with a highly organized social hierarchy, the dominant rats commanding the best nesting areas, food supplies, and breeding rights. This rat is highly intelligent, often avoiding poisoned food prepared for its extermination.

Legendary for their breeding prowess, some females may produce up to 12 litters a year, but the average is about 5. The average number of young per litter is 9, but that may vary from 6 to 22. Gestation is about 21 days and juvenile females breed at three months of age.

Probably our worst animal pest, these freeloaders destroy millions of dollars worth of food and other goods each year and are carriers of several serious diseases. Some writers claim that more human lives have been lost because of this rat than have been killed in all the wars in history.

This much despised rat occasionally disperses to the Canadian Rockies using various modes of human transportation. In 1952, for example, Norway rats arrived at Field in Yoho National Park by way of railway grain cars, but those rats were exterminated before the population could expand.

House Mouse WY

Mus musculus OLD WORLD MICE/RATS FAMILY

Another immigrant from Asia, the house mouse usually lives in close association with humans. This persistent tag-along is small with a grayish brown coat on the back, lighter gray sides, and a smoky gray belly. Weighing around 25 g (1 oz), it is approximately 17 cm (7 in) long, about half of which is tail. Its long tail is scaly and sparsely haired, its large ears almost hairless.

House mice are colonial and haunt some houses, cabins, and outbuildings in seemingly inexhaustible numbers, although some mice like to be outdoors for at least part of the year. They nest in woodpiles, cupboards, dresser drawers, mattresses, between walls, and under floors. Prolific breeders, the average litter size is about 6, the extremes being 1 to 12. Under ideal circumstances, they may breed and produce several litters throughout the year.

HOUSE MOUSE / JAN L. WASSINK

Primarily nocturnal in habit, you may hear these bold tenants scuttling about searching for nesting material, pilfering anything edible in the kitchen, romping and fighting between the walls, or scratching in the attic. The brigands leave behind little rodlike droppings as evidence of their presence. These Houdinis of the animal world can disappear in a flash by squeezing their pliable bodies through a hole no larger than a thumb.

The most familiar mouse of all, house mice are common in most townsites and in dwellings where food is available.

Meadow Jumping Mouse

N

Zapus hudsonius

JUMPING MOUSE FAMILY

Both species of jumping mice in the Canadian Rockies share a number of common characteristics. Like other saltatorial animals, such as the kangaroo, they have exceptionally long, tapering tails, twice the length of their bodies; small forefeet; long, strongly developed hind limbs; and large, outward-splayed hind feet. The long tail is essential in maintaining balance from takeoffs to landings, and in changing the direction of subsequent jumps. The legs and feet provide enough power to catapult these mice as far as 3 m (10 ft) and to a height of over 60 cm (2 ft), but normally much less; when moving at ease, the hops are only a few centimeters long. Jumping with the hind legs, they land on the forelimbs, while the rear feet come under the body for the next hop. The animal usually makes a long jump when first startled, and then rapidly hops away with a ping-pong-ball-like action, but on a zigzag course. It then "freezes" under the nearest cover, relying on camouflage, until the danger has passed. These tactics often confuse attacking predators.

Both species have tricolor bodies, although the colors differ slightly, and big black eyes. And both these elusive animals haunt similar habitat—moist meadows, sloughs, marshes, and the borders of forest brooks. Since they are adept swimmers, they are consequently taken by fish and bullfrogs, as well as by the usual predators on small mammals. Primarily nocturnal, they feed on seeds, fruits, fungi, insects, and spiders. With the shorter days of late summer, they increase their food intake and change from agile mice to obese creatures as they accumulate large quantities of body fat before hibernation. Weighing about 13 g (0.5 oz) in the spring, these little gluttons may weigh as much as 27 g (1 oz) prior to hibernation. They may remain torpid for up to eight months, curling up in little balls in their underground nests of grass.

The meadow jumping mouse has an olive brown back, the result of a mixture of black and buff hairs. The underparts are buffy white, with the back and belly being distinctly separated by pale yellow stripes. Bearing up to three litters a year, each consisting of about five offspring, these mice are occasional in the northern part of the Canadian Rockies.

MEADOW JUMPING MOUSE / JOHN GERLACH

Western Jumping Mouse

Zapus princeps

BJKCKNWY

JUMPING MOUSE FAMILY

The natural history of the western jumping mouse is similar to that of the meadow jumping mouse, apart from the fact that it produces only one litter a year. Its appearance is also similar, except the olive brown upperparts often have a dark dorsal stripe. This secretive rodent is occasional throughout our area in its preferred habitats.

Porcupine

Erethizon dorsatum

NEW WORLD PORCUPINE FAMILY

Respected for its defensive armament, cursed for its epicurean tastes, and marveled at for its sheer eccentricity, the porcupine resides in forested areas from the Mexican border to northern Alaska. Its most unique feature is the specialized defensive equipment of some 30000 quills on its back, flanks, and tail. These quills, 2.5 to 6.5 cm (1 to 2.6 in) in length, are set with tiny, scalelike barbs, and if touched with any force, will pull out of the porcupine and stick into the toucher. A porcupine has muscular control over this arsenal and raises the quills when threatened, turning itself into the zoological equivalent of a cactus. Pivoting on its front feet, the porcupine presents its back and tail to the enemy, the most damaging quills often being those studding the muscular tail as it is lashed threateningly at the attacker. Predators may succumb because the quills pierce vital organs or because they so handicap the victim that it cannot forage in normal fashion. The claim that porcupines can "throw" their quills like darts is erroneous. A "porky," in fact, is a mild-mannered mammal that would rather retreat to protective cover than fight, and it has so much faith in its deterrent advertising that it tends to go nonchalantly about its business. This insouciance is one of its striking personality traits.

This robust rodent weighs about 10 kg (22 lb); total length averages 80 cm (31 in), and the height at the shoulders is about 30 cm (12 in). It has a short, blunt-nosed face with small eyes and small, round ears. The porcupine has short powerful legs with long curved claws; it is extremely slow-footed and a strong but not agile climber. In addition to the quills, which are modified hairs, the porcupine has a dense brown undercoat with yellow-tipped guard hairs.

PORCUPINE CHEWING ON ANTLER / TOM J. ULRICH

YOUNG PORCUPINES / TOM J. ULRICH

155

Many people are intrigued about how porcupines manage to mate. Getting ready for mating, however, is more bizarre than the act itself. Once a male has established his dominance, he approaches a female with embraces and nose-rubbing. If receptive, she allows him to spray her with gouts of urine. When soaked to the proper degree, she elevates her hind quarters, flattens her quills, and twists her tail to the side, allowing the male to safely copulate. Porcupines are most raucous during the autumn mating season and vocalize with a variety of moans, screams, grunts, growls, mews, and purrs. They have a 210-day gestation period and generally produce only one offspring at a time. And they are the only North American rodent to give birth to precocious young; the newborn infant is sighted, mobile, covered with hair and quills, and quite large at birth, weighing about 500 g (1 lb). Females pugnaciously defend their territory against other females; males are much less territorial.

In summer porcupines feed on the green leaves of forbs, shrubs, and trees, while in winter they eat the cambium, buds, and twigs of trees. By feeding on the cambium layer they eventually girdle the tree, killing it by stifling the flow of nutrients. To the frustration of foresters, a single porky can damage as many as 100 valuable timber trees during a winter. Porcupines also have a ravenous appetite for salt, and will chew on any sweat-stained clothing and tools they may come across. Plywood is also particularly relished because of the glue between the layers of wood.

Because of their barbed defenses and the painful consequences they can inflict, porcupines are only occasionally preyed upon by bears, cougars, coyotes, wolves, wolverines, and great horned owls. Their most formidable foe is the fisher, and since it is particularly adept at killing porkies, it has been introduced into some commercially valuable forests.

The shortsighted and slow-moving porcupine is easy to approach once found. Cut twigs, missing patches of bark, or droppings may advertise its presence. It is fairly common in coniferous forests, especially in the subalpine zone.

Pikas, Rabbits, and Hares

(Order *Lagomorpha*)

Pikas (Family *Ochotonidae*)
Rabbits and Hares (Family *Leporidae*)

Lagomorphs were once lumped with the rodents, but they are now placed in a separate, small order of only two families. The family *Leporidae* includes the rabbits and hares, while the family *Ochotonidae* takes in the pikas. Lagomorphs have two sets of upper incisors that they use for gnawing and clipping vegetation. The first set is chisel-shaped with a deep groove on the front surface. A second set of small, peglike incisors is located directly behind the first set of uppers. The incisors grow throughout life and are selfsharpening. Chewing is done with a crosswise movement, in contrast to the rotary motion used by rodents, but as in the case of rodents, there is a distinct gap between the incisors and cheek teeth. Other general characteristics of the order include latticelike openings in the skull, and either no tail or a short one. Lagomorphs have five toes on the forefeet and four on the hind feet. Their skin is paper-thin and the fur is soft and dense.

Other physical characteristics include wide-set eyes, erect heads, long necks that swivel easily to increase the field of vision, and large ears to help detect predators. These features are less well developed in pikas.

Lagomorphs have a habit of reingesting some fecal pellets, which are ejected from the anus and then taken back into the mouth and swallowed. This practice provides nutrients, such as protein and B vitamins, that would otherwise be lost. The process of eating incompletely digested fecal pellets to ensure complete digestion is called refection. When voided again the pellets are round, hard, and dry, and are not reingested. This recycling of semidigested food in lagomorphs is similar to fermentation of forage in the larger digestive chambers of ruminants.

The terms "hare" and "rabbit" are correctly used to distinguish two different groups within the family *Leporidae*. The so-called jack rabbits and snowshoe rabbits are true hares. Hares have long ears and long legs and can run great distances; rabbits are short-eared, short-legged, and tire quickly. Baby hares enter the world fully furred, with their eyes open, and are able to hop away from danger shortly after birth; the altricial young of rabbits are born blind, furless, and helpless. Hares have their homes in clumps of grass or in nests above the ground; rabbits use burrows dug by other animals.

About 60 species of lagomorphs are recognized worldwide. Both families of the order occur in the Canadian Rockies, with the *Ochotonidae* family being represented by one species of pika and the *Leporidae* by two species of hares. There are no native rabbits in the Canadian Rockies.

Pika

Ochotona princeps

A high-pitched, kazoolike whistle or a quick movement among some rocks may signal your introduction to a pika. Vernacular names applied to this mammal include "coney" or "rock rabbit," the latter nickname being particularly appropriate since pikas are related to other lagomorphs like the rabbit, and they use rocky habitats. A pika is guinea-pig-sized, tailless, and has small, rounded ears. On average, an adult weighs about 140 g (5 oz) and is 17 cm (7 in) in length. The upperparts are generally brownish gray with rust-colored shoulders and head, and the belly is a silvery gray. The color of the pelage, however, is variable—gray in one place and cinnamon in another—to match its home talus. It has short legs with fur-cushioned feet.

Pikas are common inhabitants of talus in the alpine zone throughout all but the extreme northern limits of the Canadian Rockies. They are active only during the warmest part of the day, and if it is cold, they may not come out of their rocky maze at all. Although rock rabbits live in loosely associated colonies, each animal clearly marks its own territory. These extraordinarily chatty mammals use one call to announce their territory and another to alert members of the colony of danger. Their home in a jumble of rock is ideal since there are thousands of holes to dive into if a predator threatens. Shelter among rocks and protective coloration are the pika's only defenses against golden eagles, wolverines, and lynx. Protection from ermine and weasels is limited, however, since these animals are able to enter pika runs.

The saying make hay while the sun shines might have been coined for pikas. Because they do not hibernate in winter, pikas are constantly active in the late summer and fall gathering "hay," which they dry and then store in their burrows. Each of these rock-dwelling creatures will cut enough vegetation to make several clumps that look like miniature haystacks. Vegetation for the hay piles is cut with the teeth, carried crosswise in the mouth, and laid out to dry. If rain threatens the curing vegetation, these survival rations are quickly sheltered. Each animal jealously guards its own food supply, quickly challeng-

PIKA / TOM J. ULRICH

PIKA / TOM J. ULRICH

ing any intrusion by a neighboring animal. Fortunately, pikas are not too fussy when it comes to eating; any of the available broad-leafed greens and grasses will do. And like other members of the family, they refect their own dung.

Two litters of three to four young are born each summer. Before the onset of winter, young pikas must establish their own territories and stockpile enough rations to last until spring. Few of the second batch survive because they have so little time to meet those requirements.

These little haymakers of the mountains are difficult to see. But with a little patience, careful listening, and alertness you should be rewarded by a glimpse of a pika during your next summer hike to an alpine boulder field.

Snowshoe Hare

Lepus americanus

BJKCKNWY

RABBIT AND HARE FAMILY

Snowshoe hares are widely distributed throughout Canada in forested regions from the Arctic treeline to river bottoms and coulees on the prairies. Always in style with the seasons and offering almost perfect camouflage for each, the snowshoe's coat changes from brown in the spring to winter white in the fall. That is why this secretive creature is also known as the "varying" hare. The moderately large, black-tipped ears detect approaching enemies and help to regulate body temperature. The small tail is shaped like a powder puff. Females, larger than males, weigh about 1.5 kg (3.3 lb) and are around 46 cm (18 in) in length.

In addition to camouflage coloration, another remarkable adaptation is the large hind feet. This hare has broad, 10 to 15 cm (4 to 6 in) long hind feet that help it to achieve speeds of 40 km (25 mi) per hour over short distances, and to leap more than 2 m (6.6 ft) in a single bound. With hind toes that spread to form a broad surface, and a thick, stiff coat of winter hairs overall, these large, thickly furred feet act like snowshoes, hence the common name, allowing the animal to move easily across the snow without sinking. The distinctive track pattern, with the hind feet coming ahead of the front feet, is frequently observable in fresh snow. Sometimes you may also see a zigzag pattern left in the snow when the hare has attempted to outmaneuver a predator.

SNOWSHOE HARE IN SUMMER PELAGE / TOM J. ULRICH

Courtship begins with mating chases that may continue throughout the night. Sometime during the chase the doe accepts one or more of the train of males following her. Each doe produces an average of two to three litters per year with one to seven young per litter. They are born on the ground, usually without the benefit of a nest. Although the precocious leverets weigh only 50 g (1.8 oz) at birth, they are fully furred, open-eyed, and bushy tailed. Gaining weight rapidly, they soon become self-sufficient. The breeding season, which begins in mid-March, continues until midsummer. Within hours after parturition, a

SNOWSHOE HARE IN WINTER PELAGE / TOM J. ULRICH

female may mate again, rearing her young without male assistance.

Snowshoe hares are sedentary animals and have small home ranges. A male's realm of 6 to 7 ha (15 to 17 ac) typically overlaps those of several females, and except during the breeding season, snowshoe hares tolerate each other and often feed together in the same clearing. The domain of the snowshoe is crisscrossed with numerous well-worn trails, particularly noticeable in winter, leading between open areas where they feed and thickets where they rest for the day. Their daytime resting areas in sheltered spots are called forms. Snowshoe hares are active from dusk to dawn on a year-long basis.

Snowshoes eat a multifarious diet of forbs and grasses during the summer, shifting to the bark, buds, and branches of shrubs and trees in winter.

Several mammals go through periodic cycles of population change, with a species steadily increasing in numbers over a period of time, then suddenly crashing to very low numbers, only to rise again. The snowshoe hare cycle of about ten years is one of the best known. At the peak of the cycle, population densities of 1350 to 2500 snowshoe hares/km² (3500 to 6500 mi²) have been estimated, but these populations can crash to densities of 1 hare/km² (2.6 mi²) within a few months. Over the next several years, the population slowly returns to peak density. Lynx populations also cycle about every ten years because hares are their principal prey. Other common predators include red foxes, coyotes, mink, great horned owls, and goshawks. The snowshoe hare also suffers from a variety of infectious diseases.

The snowshoe hare is at home among both coniferous and deciduous trees, particularly in burned-over areas where there is dense new growth. It is a common forest dweller in the Rockies.

White-tailed Jack Rabbit

W

Lepus townsendii

RABBIT AND HARE FAMILY

Although commonly called a rabbit, this animal is a true hare. Like other hares, the white-tailed jack rabbit is large and slim, weighing about 4 kg (9 lb) and measuring about 60 cm (24 in) in length. Males are usually slightly smaller than females. Other hare characteristics include long, antennalike ears, long, slender legs, and a relatively long tail.

In summer, its coat is a grizzled buff, except for the white underparts, hind feet, and tail. Its ears are grizzled gray in front rimmed with white behind, and tipped with black. Its coat changes to pure white in winter, apart from the tips of the ears, which remain black.

Because of its powerful hind legs, the white-tailed jack rabbit can travel nearly 65 km (40 mi) an hour for short distances, with leaps of 4 to 6 m (13 to 20 ft). The sharp claws on its hind feet also serve as defensive weapons.

The hare's large ears help disperse excess body heat during the summer and are useful in detecting predators. Rotating each of its ears independently, the jack rabbit can pinpoint the source of a threatening sound. Should the predator come closer, the rabbit will crouch motionless, laying its ears flat against its back, thus becoming less conspicuous. If flushed, it tries to escape using its blinding speed and zigzag movements.

During the spring mating season, bucks lose their timidity and are out all hours courting females and fighting other bucks. Often deadly serious, these fights consist of biting, boxing with the forefeet, and kicking with the powerful hind legs. Shrill screams add to the drama, particularly when injuries occur. Six weeks after mating, three to six (but usually four) young are born in a shal-

WHITE-TAILED JACK RABBIT IN SUMMER / TOM J. ULRICH

162

WHITE-TAILED JACK RABBIT IN WINTER / TOM J. ULRICH

low depression, called a form, on the surface of the ground. Born well furred and with their eyes wide open, they are hopping about soon after birth and quickly learn to fend for themselves. One or two litters may be raised each summer.

The white-tailed jack rabbit's varied summer diet includes numerous wild plants and cultivated crops such as alfalfa, clover, and grain. In winter it feeds on the buds and tender twigs of many shrubs and trees, and on hay and waste grains in settled areas.

White-tailed jack rabbits, active primarily at night, are rare in the foothills of extreme southwestern Alberta, and are not present on the western slopes.

Bats

(Order *Chiroptera*)

Evening or Smooth-faced Bats
(Family *Vespertilionidae*)

Bats are the only group of mammals that have evolved the unique ability to fly. The structure that allows flight is one of nature's architectural marvels. The forelimbs have been modified by the elongation of the fingers into supports for a thin, double membrane of skin, called the patagium, that extends to the hind legs and on to the tail. Other adaptations for flight include a keeled sternum to anchor strong pectoral muscles, and elongate and tubular forelimb bones that provide both lightness and strength. These characteristics give bats aerial abilities equal to those of birds.

Bats evolved about 50 million years ago, during the early Eocene, and to date more than 900 kinds of bats have been identified. Practically worldwide in distribution, except for extremely cold polar regions and isolated islands, these creatures are the second largest group of mammals on a worldwide basis, a richness exceeded only by rodents.

Bats usually have well-furred bodies, naked, elastic membranes over the wings, large ears and chests, and narrow hips. Although bats are nocturnal, they have weak eyesight and use ultrasonic echolocation instead of vision for navigation and hunting. When bats fly, they emit 5 to 200 high-pitched cries per second, ranging in frequency from 30000 to more than 75000 cycles per second. From the echo pattern they can determine obstacles in their way, and precisely locate and capture night-flying insects, their principal prey.

With their extremely high metabolic rates, bats have to eat approximately half their body weight daily, and to satisfy these gargantuan appetites must zap about 3000 insects each night. Some people erect bat houses to take advantage of the creature's insect-eating proclivities. With heart rates of about 700 beats per minute, we might expect bats to be short-lived, but in fact, they may live an average of 4 to 8 years, and some live for more than 30 years. Their metabolism may drop to abnormally low levels as a means of conserving energy during the day and also during cold periods. In that state of torpor, they hang upside down from a sharply clawed hook near the midwing.

Some insects have developed countermeasures to avoid serving as a bat's dinner. Crickets, for example, can hear an approaching bat's "sonar" and take evasive action by changing direction or dropping to the ground. Some moths can mimic a bat's squeaks, which is like jamming the radar system, and rather than attacking the moth, the bat then veers away as if it were heading for an obstruction.

Contrary to folklore, bats are neither blind or vicious, nor do they desire to become tangled in your hair. Their sinister reputations are undeserved, and although there is public apprehension about bats as vectors of rabies, the risk is minimal. Handling them, however, is not recommended.

Eight species of bats are found in the Canadian Rockies, all of them belonging in the family *Vespertilionidae*. Their behavioral patterns vary according to species. Some are colonial during hibernation and while nursing their young; others join in small clusters; and still others are solitary. During their active period, many bats live in dense forests, while others are partial to structures, such as attics and steeples, in urban environments. Some species migrate to milder climates during the winter, while others hibernate in caves, buildings, rock crevices, or hollow trees.

Bats mate during late summer or autumn, just before hibernation, or occasionally in the spring. There is little, if any, male combat or highly demonstrative courtship. A male initiates mating by mounting and restraining the female, often producing audible calls that may pacify her. Sperm remains alive in the female's uterus until she ovulates at the end of the winter dormancy, an interval of approximately eight months. This enables her to time pregnancy independent of male courtship and to ensure that her offspring are born at the appropriate time. Female bats in our area bear only one young each year, sometime between mid-June and mid-July. Unlike other mammals, young bats are born feet first. The baby clings to mom's furry chest even when she leaves in the evening to feed, and within four or five weeks the youngster can fly on its own.

Like all mammals, bats have their enemies. Aside from human activity, which has the most detrimental impact, they are the quarry of hawks, owls, skunks, mink, weasels, marten, cats, and several others, although most predators eat bats opportunistically and not as part of their regular prey.

These characteristics, habits, and life cycle details are common to all members of the family *Vespertilionidae*. Distinguishing characteristics and other incidental details are discussed in the following individual write-ups.

Little Brown Bat

Myotis lucifugus

The little brown bat is medium-sized with pelage ranging in color from mahogany brown, through reddish brown, to pale yellowish brown. Its total length averages 9.5 cm (3.7 in) and it weighs from 8 to 12 g (0.3 to 0.4 oz) depending on the time of the year. It may be distinguished from bats of similar size by the rounded tip on its tragus (see glossary) and the lack of a keeled calcar (see glossary).

Little brown bats emerge from hibernation with the arrival of flying insects in the spring, and torpor engulfs them with the disappearance of these insects in the fall. Overwintering takes place in caves and mines; daytime roosts in the summer include caves, hollow trees, rock crevices, and buildings. Although mating occurs in the fall, fertilization is delayed until after hibernation, and only a single young is born, after a gestation period of 50 to 60 days.

This bat is common from the montane zone to treeline.

LITTLE BROWN BAT / JAN L. WASSINK

Northern Long-eared Bat

JN

Myotis septentrionalis

EVENING BAT FAMILY

As one would expect from the common name, the northern long-eared bat has large ears with a long, narrow tragus. With pelage colored reddish brown above and buffy gray below, it is a medium-sized bat, and like the little brown bat, lacks a keel on its calcar. This bat inhabits dry, coniferous forests in the northern portion of the Canadian Rockies.

NORTHERN LONG-EARED BAT / EDGAR T. JONES

Long-eared Bat

BJKWY

Myotis evotis

EVENING BAT FAMILY

The long-eared bat is another medium-sized bat with light brown pelage and striking black ears and flight membranes. It has the longest ears among the bats in the Canadian Rockies, usually greater than 2 cm (0.8 in), which may help it to find the beetles it preys on, as well as other insects. Widespread but uncommon along river valleys from Jasper southward, it occupies buildings in the summer and probably migrates south to overwinter.

Long-legged Bat

BJKW

Myotis volans

EVENING BAT FAMILY

The long-legged bat is another medium-sized bat with light to medium, reddish brown pelage. It can be distinguished from other brown, medium-sized bats by the presence of a keel on its calcar. In addition, its ears are smaller and rounder than those of the northern long-eared and little brown bats. The name of this bat derives from its relatively long tibia, but that is not obvious without careful study. Sharing many habits and life cycle characteristics with other members of the family *Vespertilionidae*, this bat is sporadically present from Jasper National Park southward, and probably migrates further south to hibernate.

California Bat K

Myotis californicus   EVENING BAT FAMILY

The California bat is yet another medium-sized brown bat, with pelage a rich, reddish brown on the upperside and a buffy brown below. It has a keeled calcar and the flight membrane is covered with fine hairs about one-third of the way down the tibia on the dorsal base. This bat is occasionally present on the southern section of the western slopes of the Canadian Rockies. It inhabits the driest portions of the montane zone in open Douglas fir forests and grassland, but likes to have ponds or flowing streams nearby.

Silver-haired Bat BJKCCKNWY

Lasionycteris noctivagans   EVENING BAT FAMILY

The silver-haired bat is migratory and relatively rare throughout the Canadian Rockies. It is medium-sized with dark brown to almost black pelage that is silver-tipped on the back and belly, but not on the head and neck. This gives it the appearance of wearing a silver-frosted cape. Its ears are short and roundish, and both ears and flight membranes are black. The tail of the membrane is covered with fine, frosted hairs about three-quarters of the way down. This bat migrates south rather than going into dormancy.

Big Brown Bat BJKCCKNWY

Eptesicus fuscus   EVENING BAT FAMILY

The big brown bat ranges in total length from 11.2 to 12.8 cm (4.4 to 5.0 in),

and has a well-defined keel on its calcar. Based on size alone, no other brown bat in our area should be confused with this creature, but despite the name, it weighs less than 28 g (1 oz). Its pelage varies from pale brown to reddish brown and the fur has a glossy luster. It is remarkably tolerant of cold temperatures, being the last to become dormant in the fall and the first to emerge in the spring. This bat is most common in townsites, particularly in old buildings and barns with accessible attics.

BIG BROWN BAT / EDGAR T. JONES

SILVER-HAIRED BAT / TOM J. ULRICH

Hoary Bat
Lasiurus cinereus

The hoary bat, the largest in the Canadian Rockies, weighs up to 35 g (1.2 oz) and has a total length of up to 14 cm (5.5 in). Its pelage is dark brown with silver-tipped hairs, giving it a handsome, frosted appearance. The underside is tawny, with a cream-colored ruff around the neck and at the base of the thumb. Both the tail and undersides of the wings are well furred. The hoary bat is a solitary, tree-dwelling species, rare in the central and southern Canadian Rockies and absent in the north.

HOARY BAT / EDGAR T. JONES

Insectivores

(Order *Insectivora*)

Shrews (Family *Soricidae*)

The order *Insectivora* consists of moles and shrews. Fossil records for this order date back to the time of the dinosaurs (Cretaceous Period). There are almost 400 recognized species worldwide in North America, northern South America, Asia, Africa, and Europe.

Insectivores, as their name implies, feed upon many forms of insects. They are rather primitive mammals, walking with the entire lower surface of the foot on the ground (plantigrade). Insectivores have long pointed snouts and short legs, with five clawed toes on each foot. In contrast, other small mammals such as mice have only four clawed toes on their forefeet. The typical tooth arrangement is three pairs of incisors, one pair of canines, four pairs of premolars, and three pairs of molars on both jaws, for a total of 44 teeth.

Only the shrew family, *Soricidae*, is found in the Canadian Rockies. Five species are known to occur there, and they are widespread. The smallest mammals in the region, all weigh less than 28 g (1 oz); one weighs only as much as a dime. Each species has a long, tapering, distinctly pointed snout, low braincase, small ears, and black eyes. The pelage is short, velvety fur. Except for their long, flexible snouts, shrews closely resemble mice. And unlike moles, shrews do only a little burrowing.

Active day and night, both summer and winter, shrews spend most of their time rummaging in forest litter or scurrying through tunnels created by other animals. With minute eyes, which are sometimes hidden in their fur, and poorly developed vision, they rely on an acute sense of hearing and smell to locate prey. Their diminutive hearts may beat from 800 to 1300 times per minute and they may breath 850 times during the same interval. Shrews have the highest metabolic rate of any mammal and are in almost constant motion, driven by their enormous appetites. These minute creatures may eat their own weight in food each day to sustain their frantic pace of life. Much of the food is used to keep themselves warm, because they have a high surface area relative to their body mass. Without food, shrews will starve to death in a few hours. They seldom live for more than 18 months.

Shrews are pugnacious. If they are not attacking fleshy insects or other invertebrates, they battle each other. A shrew can attack and kill an animal several times larger than itself, a feat accomplished by poisonous saliva. A mouse bitten and injected with a potent nerve poison dies within minutes. These aggressive predators are themselves prey to a variety of birds, fish, frogs, and small mammals.

These high-strung, diminutive creatures are loners and claim exclusive use of their domains, males and females being hostile to each other and also to members of their own sex. Mom and dad tolerate each other's company only long enough to mate, but typical of their hurried life, copulation lasts about ten seconds.

Females usually give birth two or three times over their life span. A litter ranging from two to ten, though usually around six, can be born anytime from spring to fall. The pink and hairless young, born with a single set of permanent teeth, develop rapidly and leave the nest after a few weeks.

Shrews are rarely seen by humans, and when one is, even the most experienced naturalist could not identify it to species from the quick glimpse usually afforded as the small mammal darts from one cover to another. Even in the hand, shrews are difficult to identify, skull and tooth characteristics being the only certain way to tell them apart.

The characteristics, habitats, and lifestyles detailed above generally prevail in all the shrews that may be encountered in the Canadian Rockies. Only distinguishing features and other interesting details are discussed in the individual descriptions that follow.

Masked Shrew

Sorex cinereus

BJKCKNWY

SHREW FAMILY

The masked shrew is dull brown to buffy brown above, and off-white on the lower sides, throat, and underside, with usually a yellowish tint over much of the

MASKED SHREW / JOHN SERRAO

belly. The tail is dark brown above and off-white below, with a tuft at the tip. Some individuals have a faint "mask" or darker area across the nose, hence the common name. The pelage is heavier and darker in the winter than in the summer.

Also called the "common" shrew, the masked shrew is found in a variety of habitats, including forests, grasslands, and

172

weed patches. Probably the most common shrew in our area, it occurs in both wet and quite dry areas from the valley bottom to treeline. Its diet consists of insects, earthworms, and small vertebrates such as young mice. Astoundingly, a daily food consumption of more than three times the animal's own body weight has been recorded.

Dusky Shrew
BJKCKNWY

Sorex monticolus
SHREW FAMILY

The dusky shrew is similar in coloration to the masked shrew, except for the lack of a yellow stain on the belly. It is widespread in many different habitats, but it prefers wet meadows, marshes, coniferous forests near streams, and alpine meadows. The dusky shrew is common throughout the Canadian Rockies.

Wandering Shrew

Sorex vagrans
SHREW FAMILY

The wandering shrew is a little longer and more heavily built than the masked shrew. Its pelage ranges from reddish brown to grayish in summer, while the long, silky, winter coat is a dusky color. Seldom far from water, their favorite haunts are mossy forests, willow-clad streams, horsetail stands near lakes, and sphagnum bogs. The wandering shrew's distribution in the Canadian Rockies is limited to the extreme south, the only Alberta records being from the West Castle area north of Waterton Lakes National Park.

WANDERING SHREW / JAN L. WASSINK   WANDERING SHREW PORTRAIT / JAN L. WASSINK

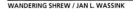

Water Shrew

Sorex palustris

The largest of the shrews in the Canadian Rockies, the water shrew has bicolored pelage of charcoal gray to blackish on the back, head, and sides, with a silvery white belly and undertail. Its broad, partly webbed hind feet are fringed with short stiff bristles along the toes, an aid in swimming. The long tail is bicolored, dark above and white below.

These adept swimmers and divers feed upon larvae and nymphs of aquatic insects such as mayfly, caddis fly, and stonefly; snails; and small fish, occasionally falling prey to larger fish themselves. Food, held down by the front feet, is grasped with the teeth and severed into pieces by vigorous upward jerks of the head. Smaller prey may be lifted up while being consumed. Food surplus to immediate needs is hoarded.

These shrews are very buoyant, floating on top of the water. They can also swim below the surface, primarily by using their large hind feet. When shrews do swim underwater or dive, air is trapped between their hairs, giving the animal a silvery appearance and reducing heat loss. The fur begins to get wet after about a minute underwater, so the shrew then pops to the surface like a cork, immediately grooming itself with its hind feet to get dry and warm.

The water shrew appears to be most frequent along cold mountain streams with abundant cover along the shorelines, although it is also found in the stagnant water of bogs and marshes. It is occasional to uncommon throughout the Canadian Rockies.

Pygmy Shrew

Sorex hoyi

The pygmy shrew, the smallest mammal in North America, may weigh no more than a dime. It is only 9 cm (3.5 in) in length, of which 3 cm (1 in) is tail, and weighs about 3 g (0.1 oz). Its pelage is a smoky brown above with grayish or paler brown underparts. The pygmy shrew looks like a smaller version of the masked shrew, and can only be positively identified by examining its unicuspid teeth. This shrew prefers drier habitat than the other shrews in the Canadian Rockies, inhabiting dry upland coniferous and deciduous forests. The status of the pygmy shrew in the Canadian Rockies is uncertain; it may be absent in the extreme south.

Glossary

Adaptation—traits an animal develops because of biological and environmental challenges.

Albinistic—whitish, having less than the normal amount of pigment.

Altricial—young that are blind and helpless at birth and require intensive care.

Arboreal—living in trees.

Calcar—a spur of bone or cartilage extending from the ankle of some bats that helps to support the tail flight membrane.

Cambium—inner bark of trees.

Canine tooth—tooth between the incisors and the premolars.

Carnassial—a pair of large opposing teeth that act as shears to cut meat and tendons.

Carnivore—flesh-eating animal.

Commensal—any species that lives with or near humans.

Crepuscular—active during periods at dawn and dusk.

Cursorial—movement by running.

Dewlap—a prominent extension of the skin of the throat, covered with hair and hanging loosely.

Diastema—a distinct gap or space between teeth.

Digitigrade—walking primarily on the toes.

Diurnal—active during the day.

Echolocation—a process in which echoes are used to locate objects.

Estrus—state of sexual excitability during which the female of most mammals will accept the male.

Fauna—the animals of a given region.

Flight (interfemoral) membrane—web of skin between the hind legs of bats, often enclosing the tail.

Food chain—a sequence of organisms on successive trophic levels—such as green plants, herbivores, and carnivores—through which energy is transferred by feeding.

Forb—a soft-stemmed, broad-leaved herb.

Form—a depression in the ground used as a nest or shelter by hares or rabbits.

Fossorial—adapted for living partially or totally underground.

Gestation—period of carrying young from conception to birth.

Gregarious—living or moving in groups.

Habitat—a particular area where an animal lives.

Harem—a group of females serviced by one male.

Herbivore—plant-eating animal.

Hibernation—the condition of decreased physical and metabolic activity assumed by certain animals during periods of unfavorable climatic conditions.

Hierarchy—a system whereby a society is comprised of levels based on the outcome of interactions that show some individuals to be dominant.

Home range—the entire area in which an individual moves around.

Incisor—front teeth between the canines.

Melanistic—blackish, having abnormal amounts of dark pigment.

Midden—piles of conifer cones, cone scales, or fodder the squirrels and other rodents collect and store for winter use.

Natatorial—movement by swimming.

Nocturnal—active in the night.

Omnivore—flesh- and plant-eating animal.

Patagium—the skin that forms the flight membranes in bats and flying squirrels.

Pelage—the covering or coat of a mammal.

Pheromone—a chemical substance that communicates information between individuals of the same species.

Plantigrade—walking on the entire foot from heel to toe.

Polygamous—having more than one mate at the same time.

Precocious—young well developed at birth and able to move about, requiring parental care for only a short period.

Predator—an animal that lives by eating other animals.

Prolific—to produce offspring abundantly.

Refection—the reingestion of incompletely digested fecal pellets, which are rechewed to ensure complete digestion.

Retractile—capable of being withdrawn into a protective sheath.

Riparian—the sides and banks of watercourses and lakes.

Rut—the annual period of sexual excitement, when a male seeks a receptive female and stays with her until mating.

Saltatorial—movement by jumping.

Scansorial—movement by climbing.

Solitary—a mammal that prefers to live alone.

Species—animals or plants exhibiting certain characteristics in common that are able to breed among themselves and produce fertile offspring.

Subnivian—in or under snow.

Talus—a sloping mass of rock fragments at the base of a cliff.

Territory—an area of habitat that an individual or group actively defends against others of the same species.

Tine—branch of an antler off the main beam.

Torpor—a state of sluggishness or inactivity to reduce energy expenditures.

Tragus—flap of skin near the bottom of the external ear opening in bats.

Underfur—thick, soft fur lying beneath longer and coarser guard hairs.

Ungulate—a mammal that walks on its toenails.

Velus—extremely fine, downy hairs.

Velvet—soft membrane of blood vessels covering newly developing antlers.

Venter—belly or abdomen.

Volant—capable of flying.

Checklist

This is a list of all mammals (Class: *Mammalia*) for the Canadian Rocky Mountains. Readers may wish to use this list to record the species they have seen.

Order *INSECTIVORA* (Moles and Shrews)
Family *Soricidae* (Shrew Family)

		B*	J	KC	K	N	W	Y
[ ] Masked Shrew	*Sorex cinereus*	X	X	X	X	X	X	X
[ ] Dusky Shrew	*S. monticolus*	X	X	X	X	X	X	X
[ ] Wandering Shrew	*S. vagrans*				Hº			H
[ ] Water Shrew	*S. palustris*	X	X	X	X	X	X	X
[ ] Pygmy Shrew	*S. hoyi*	X	X		X	X	H	H

Order *CHIROPTERA* (Bats)
Family *Vespertilionidae* (Evening or Smooth-faced Bat Family)

[ ] Little Brown Bat	*Myotis lucifugus*	X	X	X	X	X	X	X
[ ] Northern Long-eared Bat	*M. septentrionalis*		X			X		
[ ] Long-eared Bat	*M. evotis*	X	X		X	H	X	X
[ ] Long-legged Bat	*M. volans*	X	X		X		X	H
[ ] California Bat	*M. californicus*				X			
[ ] Silver-haired Bat	*Lasionycteris noctivagans*	X	X	X	X	X	X	X
[ ] Big Brown Bat	*Eptesicus fuscus*	X	X	X	X	X	X	X
[ ] Hoary Bat	*Lasiurus cinereus*	X		X	X		H	X

Order *LAGOMORPHA* (Pikas, Rabbits, and Hares)
Family *Ochotonidae* (Pika Family)

[ ] Pika	*Ochotona princeps*	X	X	X	X		X	X

Family *Leporidae* (Rabbit and Hare Family)

[ ] Snowshoe Hare	*Lepus americanus*	X	X	X	X	X	X	X
[ ] White-tailed Jack Rabbit	*L. townsendii*						X	

Order *RODENTIA* (Rodents)
Family *Sciuridae* (Squirrel Family)

[ ] Least Chipmunk	*Tamias minimus*	X	X	X	X	X	X	X
[ ] Yellow-pine Chipmunk	*T. amoenus*	X	X	X	X		X	X
[ ] Red-tailed Chipmunk	*T. ruficaudus*						X	
[ ] Woodchuck	*Marmota monax*				X	H		X
[ ] Yellow-bellied Marmot	*M. flaviventris*						X	

B* = Banff National Park, J = Jasper National Park, KC = Kananaskis Country, K = Kootenay National Park, N = Northern British Columbia, W = Waterton Lakes National Park, Y = Yoho National Park.
Hº = Hypothetical.
X¹ = Formerly present.

		B	J	KC	K	N	W	Y
[ ] Hoary Marmot	*M. caligata*	X	X	X	X	X	X	X
[ ] Richardson's Ground Squirrel	*Spermophilus richardsonii*			X		X		
[ ] Columbian Ground Squirrel	*S. columbianus*	X	X		X	X	X	X
[ ] Thirteen-lined Ground Squirrel	*S. tridecemlineatus*			X		X		
[ ] Golden-mantled Ground Squirrel	*S. lateralis*	X	X	X	X	X	X	X
[ ] Red Squirrel	*Tamiasciurus hudsonicus*	X	X	X	X	X	X	X
[ ] Northern Flying Squirrel	*Glaucomys sabrinus*	X	X	X	X	X	X	X

Family *Geomyidae*
(Pocket Gopher Family)

		B	J	KC	K	N	W	Y
[ ] Northern Pocket Gopher	*Thomomys talpoides*	H		X			X	

Family *Castoridae* (Beaver Family)

		B	J	KC	K	N	W	Y
[ ] Beaver	*Castor canadensis*	X	X	X	X	X	X	X

Family *Cricetidae*
(New World Mice/Rats Family)

		B	J	KC	K	N	W	Y
[ ] Deer Mouse	*Peromyscus maniculatus*	X	X	X	X	X	X	X
[ ] Bushy-tailed Woodrat	*Neotoma cinerea*	X	X	X	X	X	X	X
[ ] Southern Red-backed Vole	*Clethrionomys gapperi*	X	X	X	X	X	X	X
[ ] Northern Red-backed Vole	*C. rutilus*					X		
[ ] Heather Vole	*Phenacomys intermedius*	X	X	X	X	X	X	X
[ ] Meadow Vole	*Microtus pennsylvanicus*	X	X	X	X	X	X	X
[ ] Long-tailed Vole	*M. longicaudus*	X	X	X	X	X	X	X
[ ] Water Vole	*M. richardsoni*	X	X	X	H		X	X
[ ] Muskrat	*Ondatra zibethicus*	X	X	X	X	X	X	X
[ ] Brown Lemming	*Lemmus sibiricus*					X		
[ ] Northern Bog Lemming	*Synaptomys borealis*	X	X	X	X	H	H	X

Family *Muridae*
(Old World Mice/Rats Family)

		B	J	KC	K	N	W	Y
[ ] Norway Rat	*Rattus norvegicus*						X[1]	
[ ] House Mouse	*Mus musculus*	H	H				X	X

Family *Zapodidae*
(Jumping Mouse Family)

		B	J	KC	K	N	W	Y
[ ] Meadow Jumping Mouse	*Zapus hudsonius*					X		
[ ] Western Jumping Mouse	*Z. princeps*	X	X	X	X	X	X	X

Family *Erethizontidae*
(New World Porcupine Family)

		B	J	KC	K	N	W	Y
[ ] Porcupine	*Erethizon dorsatum*	X	X	X	X	X	X	X

Order *CARNIVORA* (Carnivores)

Family *Canidae* (Dog Family)

		B	J	KC	K	N	W	Y
[ ] Coyote	*Canis latrans*	X	X	X	X	X	X	X
[ ] Gray Wolf	*C. lupus*	X	X	X	X	X	X	X
[ ] Red Fox	*Vulpes vulpes*	X	X	X	X	X	X	X

Family *Ursidae* (Bear Family)

		B	J	KC	K	N	W	Y
[ ] Black Bear	*Ursus americanus*	X	X	X	X	X	X	X
[ ] Grizzly Bear	*U. arctos*	X	X	X	X	X	X	X

		B	J	KC	K	N	W	Y
Family *Procyonidae* (Raccoon Family)								
[ ] Raccoon	*Procyon lotor*		X				X	
Family *Mustelidae* (Weasel Family)								
[ ] Marten	*Martes americana*	X	X	X	X	X	X	X
[ ] Fisher	*M. pennanti*	X	X	X	X	X	H	X
[ ] Ermine	*Mustela erminea*	X	X	X	X	X	X	X
[ ] Least Weasel	*M. nivalis*	X	X	X	H	X	X	X
[ ] Long-tailed Weasel	*M. frenata*	X	X	X	H		X	X
[ ] Mink	*M. vison*	X	X	X	X	X	X	X
[ ] Wolverine	*Gulo gulo*	X	X	X	X	X	X	X
[ ] Badger	*Taxidea taxus*	X		X	X		X	H
[ ] Striped Skunk	*Mephitis mephitis*		X	X	X	X	X	X
[ ] River Otter	*Lutra canadensis*		X	X	X	X	X	X
Family *Felidae* (Cat Family)								
[ ] Cougar	*Felis concolor*	X	X	X	X	X	X	X
[ ] Canada Lynx	*Lynx canadensis*	X	X	X	X	X	X	X
[ ] Bobcat	*L. rufus*			X	X	X	X	H

Order *ARTIODACTYLA*
(Deer, Pronghorn, and Bovids)

		B	J	KC	K	N	W	Y
Family *Cervidae* (Deer Family)								
[ ] Wapiti or Elk	*Cervus elaphus*	X	X	X	X	X	X	X
[ ] Mule Deer	*Odocoileus hemionus*	X	X	X	X	X	X	X
[ ] White-tailed Deer	*O. virginianus*	X	X	X	X	X	X	X
[ ] Moose	*Alces alces*	X	X	X	X	X	X	X
[ ] Woodland Caribou	*Rangifer tarandus*	X	X			X		
Family *Antilocapridae* (Pronghorn Family)								
[ ] Pronghorn	*Antilocapra americana*							
Family *Bovidae* (Bovid Family)								
[ ] Bison	*Bison bison*	X	X[1]			X	X	
[ ] Mountain Goat	*Oreamnos americanus*	X	X	X	X	X	X	X
[ ] Bighorn Sheep	*Ovis canadensis*	X	X	X	X	X	X	X
[ ] Thinhorn Sheep	*O. dalli*					X		

Selected References

*Alberta wildlife viewing guide.*1990. Edmonton, Alberta: Lone Pine Publishing.

Albone, E.S. 1984. *Mammalian semiochemistry: The investigation of chemical signals between mammals.* Chichester, Great Britain: John Wiley and Sons.

Banfield, A.W.F. 1974. *The mammals of Canada.* Toronto, Ontario: University of Toronto Press.

Carbyn, L.N. 1983. *Wolves in Canada and Alaska: Their status, biology, and management.* Canadian Wildlife Service Report Series, no. 45. Ottawa, Ontario: Queen's Printer.

Chadwick, D.H. 1983. *A beast the color of winter.* San Francisco, California: Sierra Club Books.

Chapman, J.A., and G.A. Feldhamer (eds). 1982. *Wild mammals of North America.* Baltimore, Maryland: The Johns Hopkins University Press.

Cowan, I. McT., and C.J. Guiguet. 1956. *The mammals of British Columbia.* Victoria, British Columbia: British Columbia Provincial Museum.

Flook, D.R. 1970. *A study in sex differential in the survival of wapiti.* Canadian Wildlife Service Report Series, no. 11. Ottawa, Ontario: Queen's Printer.

Gadd, B. 1995. *Handbook of the Canadian Rockies.* 2nd ed. Jasper, Alberta: Corax Press.

Geist, V. 1971. *Mountain sheep: A study in behavior and evolution.* Chicago, Illinois: University of Chicago Press.

———. 1993. *Wild sheep country.* Minocqua, Wisconsin: Northword Press, Incorporated.

Geist, V., and F. Walther. 1974. *The behaviour of ungulates and its relation to management.* IUCN Publication New Series, no. 24. Morges, Switzerland.

Halls, L.K. (ed). 1984. *White-tailed deer ecology and management.* Harrisburg, Pennsylvania: Stackpole Books.

Harrington, F., and P. Paquet (eds). 1982. *Wolves of the world: Perspectives of behavior, ecology, and conservation.* Park Ridge, New Jersey: Noyes Publications.

Herrero, S. 1985. *Bear attacks: Their causes and avoidance.* Piscataway, New Jersey: Winchester Press.

Holroyd, G.L., and K.J. Van Tighem. 1983. *Ecological (biophysical) land classification of Banff and Jasper national parks.* Vol. 3, *The wildlife inventory.* Edmonton, Alberta: Environment Canada.

Keith, L.B. 1963. *Wildlife's ten-year cycle.* Madison, Wisconsin: University of Wisconsin Press

McCrory, W.P., and D.A. Blood. 1978. *An inventory of the mammals of Yoho National Park, British Columbia.* Calgary, Alberta: Parks Canada, Western Region.

Mitchell, G.J. 1980. *The pronghorn antelope in Alberta.* Regina, Saskatchewan: University of Regina Press.

Murie, O.J. 1975. *A field guide to animal tracks.* The Peterson Field Guide Series. Boston, Massachusetts: Houghton Mifflin Co.

Nagorsen, D.W. 1990. *The mammals of British Columbia.* Royal British Columbia Museum Memoir, no. 4. Vancouver, British Columbia: Royal British Columbia Museum.

Nagorsen, D.W., and R.M. Brigham. 1993. *Bats of British Columbia.* The mammals of British Columbia, vol. 1. Vancouver: UBC Press.

Nielsen, P.L. 1973. *The mammals of Waterton Lakes National Park, Alberta.* Edmonton, Alberta: Environment Canada, Canadian Wildlife Service.

Peterson, R.L. 1955. *North American moose.* Toronto, Ontario: University of Toronto Press.

Poll, D.M., M.M. Porter, G.L. Holroyd, R.M. Wershler, and L.W. Gyug. 1984. *Ecological land classification of Kootenay National Park, British Columbia.* Vol. 2, *Wildlife resource.* Edmonton, Alberta: Environment Canada.

Reynolds, H.W., R.D. Glaholt, and A.W.L. Hawley. 1982. "Bison." In *Wild mammals of North America,* ed. J.A. Chapman and G.A. Feldhamer. Baltimore, Maryland: The Johns Hopkins University Press.

Roe, F.G. 1951. *The North American buffalo.* Toronto, Ontario: University of Toronto Press.

Russell, R.H., J.W. Nolan, N.A. Woody, and G. Anderson. 1979. *A study of the grizzly bear* (Ursus arctos L.) *in Jasper National Park, 1975–1978.* Edmonton, Alberta: Environment Canada, Canadian Wildlife Service.

Schmidt, J.L., and D.L. Gilbert. 1978. *Big game of North America: Ecology and management.* Harrisburg, Pennsylvania: Stackpole Books.

Scotter, G.W., and H. Flygare. 1986. *Wildflowers of the Canadian Rockies.* Edmonton, Alberta: Hurtig Publishers.

Scotter, G.W., T.J. Ulrich, and E.T. Jones. 1990. *Birds of the Canadian Rockies.* Saskatoon, Saskatchewan: Western Producer Prairie Books.

Sebeok, T.A. (ed). 1977. *How animals communicate.* Bloomington, Indiana: Indiana University Press.

Smith, H.C. 1993. *Alberta mammals: An atlas and guide.* Edmonton, Alberta: Provincial Museum of Alberta.

Smith, W.J. 1977. *The behavior of communicating.* Cambridge, Massachusetts: Harvard University Press.

Stelfox, B., S. Wasel, and L. Hunt. 1992. *Field guide to the hoofed mammals of Jasper and Banff national parks.* Jasper, Alberta: Parks and People.

Stelfox, J.B. (ed). 1993. *Hoofed mammals of Alberta.* Edmonton, Alberta: Lone Pine Publishing.

Thomas, J.W., and D.E. Toweill (eds). 1982. *Elk of North America.* Harrisburg, Pennsylvania: Stackpole Books.

Ulrich, T.J. 1986. *Mammals of the northern Rockies.* Missoula, Montana: Mountain Press Publishing Company.

van Zyll de Jong, C.G. 1983. *Handbook of Canadian mammals.* Part 1, *Marsupials and insectivores.* Ottawa, Ontario: National Museum of Natural Sciences.

———. 1985. *Handbook of Canadian mammals.* Part 2, *Bats.* Ottawa, Ontario: National Museum of Natural Sciences.

Wallmo, O.C. 1981. *Mule and black-tailed deer of North America.* Lincoln, Nebraska: University of Nebraska Press.

Walther, F.R. 1984. *Communication and expression in hoofed mammals.* Bloomington, Indiana: Indiana University Press.

Wareham, B., G. Whyte, and S. Kennedy. 1991. *British Columbia wildlife viewing guide.* Edmonton, Alberta: Lone Pine Publishing.

Index

About the Authors

George W. Scotter

Born and raised in the shadows of the Rockies in southern Alberta, George Scotter credits frequent family visits to the mountains with stimulating an early interest in nature that developed into a lifelong vocation. He has lived and worked in or near the Rockies throughout his life, much of that time having been spent prying into the private lives of native mammals.

With formal training in botany, ecology, taxonomy, and wildlife management, Dr. Scotter has worked in many capacities for the Canadian Wildlife Service of Environment Canada for more than 30 years, serving as a wildlife biologist, research scientist, and director of wildlife research based in Edmonton, Alberta. He was also an adjunct professor in Forest Science at the University of Alberta and the Natural Resources Institute, University of Manitoba.

George Scotter has written three books and contributed more than 150 articles, mainly on aspects of natural history in western and northern Canada, to major scientific journals and popular magazines, including *Canadian Geographic*, *Nature Canada*, and *North*. Vice-president and later president of the Canadian Nature Federation, he is an active member of several other conservation groups, and was the 1985 winner of the prestigious J.B. Harkin medal, awarded for outstanding contributions toward conservation.

Now retired, George and his wife, Etta, live in Kelowna, British Columbia.

Tom J. Ulrich

Born in Chicago, Illinois, Tom Ulrich completed undergraduate and graduate work at Southern Illinois University. During a four-year period of teaching high school biology, he spent his summer vacations traveling through national parks all over the United States and Canada. On one visit to Glacier National Park, Tom developed a particular admiration and love for mountain goats.

Retiring from teaching in 1975, Tom purchased camera gear and migrated to Glacier, where he spent several seasons observing and photographing mountain goats, thus launching his career as a wildlife photographer. Over the past 20 years Tom has spent extended periods of time in the outdoors capturing numerous bird and mammal species on film. His photographs have appeared in such publications as *Ranger Rick*, *National Wildlife*, *Audubon*, *American Hunter*, *Alaska Magazine*, and numerous others. He won the National Wildlife Photo Contest in 1979 and 1981, and in 1987 was named International Wildlife Photographer of the Year for a photograph of a pair of polar bears playfighting. Tom is a frequent visitor to the Canadian Rockies. He and his dog, Buddie, live in Montana just outside Glacier National Park.